Torn. Torn says it all. Though I walked through so much of Alison and Nathan's story from a distance, I didn't 'live' it until I read Torn. When things are torn, they are not a clean cut or tear. They are usually ripped, making it impossible to put back together in a way that it looks as good as new. Not only did this family live this with honor and grace, even in the most unbelievably trying times, testing of their faith and ability, you would never know today what they have lived through. Their story, this lived out testimony, will challenge you, strengthen you and encourage you. It is in the pit of despair and complete desperation, with nowhere to go or look but 'UP', that you find God in ways you could never know Him. We are to share in the sufferings of Christ, something that is seldom taught in the Church. The Atwoods' suffering, their trials and their victories have made them purer, more devoted followers of Christ and warriors. It is an honor to know them and to be their Aunt Nancy.

Nancy Lovelace, Executive Director
Go To Nations, Jacksonville, FL

i

TORN

Building Resilience Through Crisis and Recovery

Alison Vaughn Atwood

ISBN: 978-1-7361605-2-7

Printed in the United States of America

Cover Design: Nathan William Atwood

Published by Go To Nations Publishing
3771 Spring Park Road
Jacksonville, FL 32207

DEDICATION

First and foremost, I dedicate this book to the Lord. This is His story of victory, for He alone can bring the victory. It was by the power of the Holy Spirit that I was able to put into words one of the hardest battles of my life yet continue to find healing, and for that I am so grateful.

This book is also dedicated to my family: my incredibly patient and loving husband of 20 years, Nathan, and our four anointed and gifted children, Ethan, Bethany, Gabriel and Camila. This is not just my journey. It is my perspective, but it includes experiences that are shaping our family and forming our legacy. I thank God for each of them and pray that through the generations, this testimony of the Lord's goodness in our lives will be told and retold.

CONTENTS

PREFACE

When this season of our lives began, I knew it would be the most difficult time we had ever faced up until that point. I also knew there would be a day that God would call upon me to write down the testimony of the battle that He victoriously brought us through. As you read you will see what some of those testimonies are for me personally; however, we all have our own battles and testimonies that await. That is how we overcome. As Christ followers we are called to a life of testimonies. We are called to a life of resiliently and passionately pursuing the Father's heart and will for our lives, no matter the cost, and there is always a cost in the natural for things that are won in the spiritual. Although we are not called to an easy life, we are called to overcome, and with Him we already have.

Then I heard a loud voice saying in heaven, "Now salvation, and strength, and the kingdom of our God, and the power of His Christ have come, for the accuser of our brethren, who accused them before our God day and night, has been cast down. And they overcame him by the blood of the Lamb and by the word of their testimony, and they did not love their lives to the death."
Revelation 12:10-11 (NKJV)

PREPARING FOR CRISIS

———◆———

THE AIRPORT

I unsuccessfully pushed back tears as they rolled down my cheeks and the saltiness into my mouth. I was still in shock. *How did we get here? I can't believe this is my life.* Normally I would start a conversation with the person in the seat next to me in the plane, but today I just felt like I couldn't get a word out without choking up. So instead, I stared out the window as the flight attendants gave instructions, and I prayed for God to rescue us. I prayed for Him to do a miracle, and I believed that He would.

It was my first flight back to Honduras alone. I realized in those few hours as I traveled thousands of miles away from North Carolina, where I had just left my husband and two of my children, that my life would never be the same. I was about to embark on something that until that point had never even been a thought, and I wasn't sure that I was ready.

When I arrived at the gate, Gabriel and Camila joyfully ran to me after a month of separation. I could see it in their deep brown eyes that they didn't understand why their father and siblings were not with me. Tears ran down all our faces once more. I took a deep breath and realized right then that this would be the hardest thing I had ever faced, and I couldn't do it alone.

WALKING INTO A NEW SEASON

In May 2017, my husband Nathan and I, who had been serving as full-time missionaries in Central America since 2012, were serving as team leaders to a growing team of missionaries. We had successfully led two internships at the time and had a handful of missionaries whom we had the privilege of leading. However, we sensed that God was calling us into a new season and a new assignment. We had been seeking God about whether that meant partnering with another organization a few hours away from where we lived. Their ministry was to women and children who had been victims of physical or sexual violence. Nathan and I were able to get a trusted friend and fellow missionary to watch our four children for the weekend so that we could travel down to visit this ministry; however, after packing all of our belongings into our Honda Pilot, the previously working vehicle would not start. We worked on it a while to no avail. We pondered on taking our director's vehicle, which they had generously offered for us to use, but we both felt it was God who was creating the blockade, so we cancelled the trip. Since we rarely afforded time away by ourselves, we instead decided to take the couple nights to stay at a nearby hotel. That night we spent time in prayer before the Lord, and within a short amount of time He spoke to both our hearts. We both quickly realized that He was speaking a new word and it took both of us by surprise. He was preparing our family for transition back to the United States. Of course, that would take God mightily moving in our lives. Our two foster children would need to complete their adoption processes first to migrate to the United States, and although we knew that would take some time, we had no idea just how long that would take.

MY DAD

I was accustomed to not living close to family. I got married at 19 and lived at least two hours away from my family most of the time since, but one of the most exciting aspects about the vision the Lord had given us was the thought of being closer to family again. So, needless to say, I was thrilled to tell my dad in May that we would be moving once the adoptions were complete.

I was looking forward to talking to him and my mom about it in-person when I booked my flight to North Carolina for June. During that season of life, I made it home to see my family once every year or two, and my last visit home was divinely coordinated with my dad's emergent visit to the hospital for a gallbladder rupture. I became aware of the fact that the Lord was strategic in His planning, and this next visit cemented that belief.

I landed at the airport with my daughter Bethany around midnight. We were tired from the trip but relieved to be on American soil once again. We slept well that night, slept in the following morning, and went to lunch with my mother-in-law, with whom we were staying. As we drove back to her home the phone rang, and it was my sister. She was frantic on the other line. My dad had been transported to the hospital last midnight, around the time I had landed at the airport, and was in route to a larger hospital forty-five minutes away via ambulance. His heart had stopped, and they were trying to get him back. She called to tell me they didn't expect him to make it. I immediately said, "Not today. I'm on my way." I hung up the phone, borrowed my mother-in-law's car, and began the drive. In the car, I began to do something I had never done before: I waged war on the spirit of death. I prayed in the spirit fervently most of the way there until, suddenly, I felt something shift. I felt a lightness, and I began to praise God. I realized something significant had happened. My father, who had never openly professed Jesus, had been the center of not only my prayers but our whole family's for many, many years, and God had me there for such a time as this. When I got there, I was informed that he had died and remained without a heartbeat for twenty minutes before his heart started beating again. He was on a ventilator, but he was alive. The time of his cardiac arrest miraculously coordinated with my prayers, and God had shown mercy and brought resurrection power back into his body.

I was mostly by my dad's side for the next seven days. I knew I was there to pray over him, declare God's promises, and bring him comfort. I got to see the tear roll from his eye, even though he was unconscious, as I told him about how much the Lord loved him. Eventually, I had decided to step away from the hospital to spend a night with my daughter at my mother-in-law's house. I was on my way back to the hospital the next morning when I got the call. I was ten minutes away from the hospital when they told me that his heart had stopped again, and this time they could not revive him. My heart was broken. I had believed for the last week for life to come back into his body, but God opened my eyes to the miraculous nature of those seven days. I believe my dad overcame death through the blood of Jesus and encountered the inheritance that God had for him.

A DEEP WELL

This was not the first time that I experienced the loss of a family member — I had suddenly lost my brother while in my twenties — but that day, there was something that changed within me, something that I suspect happens to most when they lose a parent. My worldview changed. My heart changed. I could see every detail of God's goodness pouring down into my situation. He had divinely brought me in to stay by my father's side, to fight for him, to war for him, and to remind him of God's truths in his last days. I felt honored by God himself, but I felt all the loss. I was finally going to be moving back to North Carolina to spend time with him and my mom, and he would get to meet his two newest grandchildren, but that didn't happen. My spirit told me that God's goodness is not contingent on our circumstances, but my heart was angry. It was my first time becoming angry with the Lord, and I cried out to him and said, "I have done all that you asked of me. I left everything to serve you, and you use me like a pawn on a chess board, just to get what you want. But what about what I want?" I immediately felt a conflict between my spirit and flesh and asked for forgiveness, but it didn't take the feelings away.

Soon after, I reached out to a trusted friend. She led me into inner healing to seek the Father's heart, and what the Lord spoke to my spirit will stay with me forever: "My daughter, you are not a pawn on my chessboard, but I have created you as a deep well. You love and feel deeply, and you allow Me to pour my living water into you and then give it out. My heart is not to hurt you, but for you." Instantly, my anger and frustration faded. I repented, and I walked away freer with a new perspective and identity. Because of that encounter, I began longing for the Lord like never before, and my faith was ignited. What came next was truly supernatural.

THE FALL OF 2017

After that revelation, I felt something shift, and the Lord took me into a new season. It was a pivotal time for me. It was a time in which either I could have chosen to stay in my emotions, my anger, and justify it, or I could seek Him for the greater truth. I chose the latter. We did not enroll our two eldest children for school again that fall but began to homeschool. Nathan and I decided not to host another missionary internship the following year and slowed things down as much as we could in our busy lives. It was during this time that the Lord spoke to me to get up at 4:30am each morning, just to be with him. I had always been a morning person, but this was a whole new level. It was mid-September, and it started with Nehemiah. I remember being on the couch downstairs in our home that was already 80°F before sunrise, drinking my coffee and reading the Bible, and I began to journal. The Lord began to give me words faster than I could type them. That began the most supernatural outpouring of revelation, visions, and prophetic words I had ever experienced, and for the next three months, I literally felt like I was in the arms of God. Our family started praying for one another and making declarations, and we all embraced a new dependency on God. We fervently started praying for God to heal my husband's kidneys that had been ravaged by an autoimmune disease, for our foster children to be released by a broken government into our family for adoption, and for the healing of the nations.

I also started praying new prayers, that I have since learned transform lives. I prayed for a heart

like David, for obedience like Ezekiel, that my heart would be circumcised, that my emotions would be healed and not allowed to rule me, and that most of all, God's will, God's way, would be accomplished in our lives. But when God started to move and answer those prayers, it looked nothing like the miraculous events that I had imagined would unfold.

Journal Entry, September 18, 2017

Thank you, Father, that in You is all eternity, and every good and perfect thing comes down from the Father of Lights. Thank you, Father, that you have called us for such a time as this. A pivotal time in history where You, our gracious Father, are rebuilding Your church and the nations to reflect Your glory. Just as Nehemiah was sent to rebuild the walls of Jerusalem, You are sending your people to do a great work. I pray Father that we will be sensitive to the leading of Your Spirit, heeding Your advice on when to gather materials, when to present ourselves before the leaders of the land, when to fight and when to rest. I declare that as you have sent us as Your righteous heirs that our lives are holy and blameless before you, Oh King. That we are sent not only as the meek among the poor, but bold conquerors among the kings of this world to re-establish

Your holy city and regain ground that the enemy has unjustly stolen. I pray Father that you will continue to confuse the plans of the enemy and all those who oppose You and Your anointed. We refuse to live under the corrupt legal system of the enemy who seeks to kill, steal, and destroy, sending foxes into the gaps of the fences, but instead the fences are being made stronger and You alone are glorified. We commit ourselves to standing guard against the tactics of the enemy and pray Father that you will give us eyes to see and ears to hear from your Holy Spirit. We work with one hand and war with the other. We take on the whole armor of God and wage war against the unjust, the unholy, the corruption and hate and declare we will see justice reign — in our families, the church, the governments, the nations — there is nothing that does not belong to You, Father. You who use the earth as a footstool and from whose very breath we were created, we pray that all that was created from You returns to You, and this is a season for restoration and a returning to Your Holy City. I thank you Father that you fight for us, and the war has been won!

Journal Entry, October 25, 2017

"*Fear not my child. I have not given you a spirit of fear, but of power, love, and a sound mind. Your destiny and that of your children is already settled in heaven. It is a promise that is already done, and I knew the steps you would take. You have not strayed from my word or my heart. I will give you abundant grace and favor, and you will overcome. The covenants of the land are not covenants that I hold myself to. I am free from that and so are you as you live in me. Continue to grow and learn. I am bringing you deeper and this time, fear will not overcome you. This time the enemy will not keep you from what I have for you. You will push into the hard things and your emotions you will not hide from me. I love you my daughter, and I love your children, whom I sent. Their destinies and futures are mine.*"

Journal Entry, November 23, 2017

Oh Father, how I praise You today and give thanks for Your faithfulness and goodness. Today and every day I celebrate You in your majesty and splendor. Everyday that I live and breathe in Your presence is a joy and there is a supernatural peace residing in my soul. Father, I thank You for many rich blessings today and how You continue to lavish upon me more and more of You, Your presence, Your revelation. My prayer today is that I would continue to go deeper into the destiny that You have for me. Where I am ankle or knee deep may I go into shoulder deep and may the living waters that flow from Your very being engulf me. May I be overwhelmed by Your presence and goodness that surrounds me. Use me Father to bring healing to the nations. Define my vision, make my path straight and may my thoughts not stray from that which You have for me. May I bear fruit in season and out, for 12 months, as I am planted with deep roots next to the river of life. May my heart not fail as Your Holy Spirit advocates and comforts me in the midst of battle. May I lean not onto my own understanding, but continually seek insight into Your mysteries and deep things. Holy Spirit, the revealer of truth from the Father, speak to me and may my eyes be open to see, ears to hear and heart to perceive. Grow my character and love for You and Your people. I pray a supernatural release of love and abundant grace for this season. Wisdom to move with honor and grace into this next season. I want all that You have for me, all that You destined for me, and I won't relent until You have it all. I love you Father.

I felt Jesus was saying to me today that He wants me to rest like Elijah — eat and rest. The journey is too much. He has prepared for me a great task ahead, and in this season, I am to rest and eat. He will prepare me for what is ahead, and I will have heavenly food and drink to sustain me.

COUNTRY UNDER SEIGE

During the fall of 2017, when God was pouring out His Spirit, the counterattacks were almost innumerable. Within those short three months, my health was declining rapidly. I had a recurrent urinary tract infection that took a total of six months and multiple antibiotics to treat, one of which caused me to experience an allergic reaction. I was told during this time by a neurologist after CT and MRI imaging that I had two cysts on my spine, two herniated disks, and that the myelin sheath was deteriorating on my spine, leading to symptoms that mimicked multiple sclerosis. Leg pain that I had been experiencing for years rapidly accelerated to the point where I was bed bound certain days. Also, during that time, my son Gabriel, three at the time, suffered a hairline fracture to the skull after running into a stone wall. The wound reopened three times after closure at the hospital, which necessitated more hospital visits. My fifteen-year-old son Ethan had sudden curvature of his spine leading to a depression in his sternum and scoliosis. Probably one of the most debilitating issues at the time was our political climate.

We moved to San Pedro Sula, Honduras, in May 2014. At the time, it was considered the murder capital of the world per capita, and it was not completely uncommon to see dead bodies on or near the highways. I had to work my heart not to become desensitized by the stories of violence. We spent several years ministering to the poorest neighborhoods through teaching, evangelism, children's ministry and medical, many times while the gangs followed us around "their" neighborhoods. We were no stranger to risky situations, but this would be our first election to live through in Honduras, and our circumstances felt even more uncertain. Among a tired and oppressed people, the emotions were evident on every side, and my regular trip to the grocery store became a time to stock up on can goods, water, and essential supplies. Highways were being blockaded, cars were hit with bricks and set on fire, portions of neighborhoods were looted and burned. Gangs were breaking into neighborhoods and ransacking houses, taking advantage of the unrest. We were alerted several times that neighborhood guards apprehended those attempting to do the same in our neighborhood. We moved our children out of their individual bedrooms, and everyone slept on mattresses in our bedroom in the event that we would have a break-in during the night. Fear was so thick, it could have been cut with a knife, yet God sustained our faith and even graced us with supernatural peace. Then came the day I thought would never come.

THE DAY OF DISBELIEF

Nathan was diagnosed with kidney disease in January 2004. He was only twenty-six years old, and I was twenty-one. Ethan was a toddler at the time, and we were young Christians. We had both given our hearts to the Lord on the same day in 2001, four weeks after getting married. We were on fire for the Lord and zealous for Him, so when the diagnosis of Stage 3 renal failure was given, it felt easy to trust in God. The doctor said at the time that they would start preparing him for dialysis soon, but we had other plans, and we made it clear that God was going to heal Nathan. That kind of faith is rarely welcomed in the medical community, but it proved to be real. Weekly visits at the time turned monthly, and then quarterly, and then semiannual, with no progression of the disease and Nathan's body sustaining well with the functioning thirty percent it had left. The doctor reiterated that Nathan's disease is progressive, and there was no way to explain the "remission" of the disease. However, we knew who was sustaining Nathan, and ultimately, I felt he knew too. In 2010, we had a different conversation with Nathan's kidney doctor and asked him to help us coordinate a move to Guatemala. I remember him saying that normally he would be against any patient with Nathan's condition moving overseas, but nothing was normal about what the Lord was doing in Nathan. He helped to coordinate his medications, so that we could relocate our family and follow God's destiny for our lives.

We never gave up believing, and still to this day do not, for the miraculous healing of his kidneys. We never even entertained the thoughts of sudden disaster or dialysis. We never talked about kidney transplant because we just knew that God was going to do the impossible, and He had already sustained him for fourteen years when the doctors gave him originally only months. ***So, imagine our shock when the doctor told us that Nathan was in complete kidney failure.***

It was two days before Ethan's fifteenth birthday. Due to my ongoing urinary tract infection and back pain, I had been sent for a kidney ultrasound. The doctor found a cyst on my kidney while doing the ultrasound and sent me to a nephrologist for treatment. The nephrologist wanted to send me for a CT, but since the hospital was across town, I had Nathan come with me. There were still riots and spontaneous blockades, so he came with me for safety. After the CT scan we traveled back to the nephrologist. To my surprise, he explained that the cyst was gone, and then I realized that the pain had disappeared as well. It was perplexing to me at the time, but I now know it was God's way of getting Nathan where he needed to be. While at the doctor's office, we told him of Nathan's history, and he recommended Nathan having lab work done. Since we were close to his normal time for having lab work done, we stopped by the lab, which was in the same plaza, before going home. I remember getting the email with his results and casually opening it up, expecting it to be the same as it always was. But it wasn't. It was far from normal, and so our first reaction was to believe the lab was wrong. He went back again the next day, getting out before lunch in order to avoid riots, but the results were the same. We found ourselves in the doctor's office later that day hearing the doctor say, ***"You need to start dialysis immediately. Your kidneys have completely failed."***

I remember waking up at 4:30am the next morning on my son's birthday. I felt like I had a ton of bricks on my back, but God allowed me to push into new levels of faith that could have only been given as a gift of grace. I chose to speak the opposite of what I felt in my emotions, but I knew that He alone would have to rescue us.

Journal Entry, December 7, 2017

Lord, we exalt you today and praise Your wonderful name. We shout to the world all Your wonderful deeds and the love of your being. You are worthy of all praise, glory, and honor. I declare your love and your words over Nathan, over our entire family and say that we are a family that is blessed of the Lord. You, oh Father, guide the steps of the righteous and You do not allow us to falter. Just as You care for the birds of the air, even more You care for and lovingly bind the wounds of Your children. We choose to hold to Your promises today and hold firm in faith and perseverance, knowing that You remain on Your throne. You have not changed, nor Your heart to heal your people. I declare a new season of health and prosperity over our family today in Jesus' name. A new season of increased favor and double portion. Double portion not only of health but of love, wisdom, understanding, compassion, all Your gifts that You have for us. I declare that we will stand on Your word and not man's. We will not fear bad news, but our hope will remain in You. You said that we can ask for anything in Your name, and it will be given. We ask for restoration in our family's health and a giving back of what has been stolen from our bodies in Jesus' name. We are believing that our youth be restored and You, oh Lord, sustain the temples of your Holy Spirit. I send out warring angels to overtake the forces of the enemy and break down all strongholds of fear, intimidation, disease and infirmity in our lives in Jesus' name. Father, we repent for any idolatry, ways in which we have put other things or other's opinions above Yours, for not seeking Your face and Your wisdom first. However, we are determined to go deeper in You, Father. To jump into the deep waters with you. Your will your way. To fellowship and commune with You on a new level, and our faith will grow. We ask for an outpouring of joy and for faith to rise up within our souls. Father, you said that faith as a mustard seed moves mountains. We speak to the mountain of kidney disease, of IgA nephropathy, of any diseases that are inflicting our families and say that they are thrown into the ocean, never to rise again. We ask for an open door to walk through the new season that you have for us, but that we will take the testimonies and the experiences in which we have proven victorious through Christ with us, to speak forever of your marvelous works. As for me and my house, we are blessed of the Lord, with long life, health, and an ability to go into the deep, intimate places with you our God, whom we love with all our heart. You are always good, and we praise you. Amen!

ON OUR WAY OUT

Within a few days, we had made the decision that
Nathan, Ethan, Bethany, and I would travel back to the
US to get a second opinion. We were still not fully
convinced that this was our reality, but we made the last-
minute decision to visit Bethel Church in Redding,
California, before flying into North Carolina. We
thought, *God will surely heal him there, and we won't have to
make that hard decision.* It was our first time leaving
Gabriel and Camila for more than a couple of nights, for
they legally could not legally leave Honduras as foster
children. It was heartbreaking.

I still remember the last day our whole family was
together in December 2017. Gabriel and Camila were
only three years old then, but they knew something was
different. They asked if we could play on the trampoline
one more time before we left. It was one of their
favorite things to do with us. We had our luggage packed
at the door. We went outside, and Nathan crawled up on
the trampoline with the kids while I watched. Gabriel
and Camila grinned ear-to-ear while their daddy jumped
with them one more time, tossing them into the air, not
knowing that would be the last time to see him face to
face for a long time. Then we settled into the car. We

pushed back tears as we silently peered out the windows, vigilantly watching for roadblocks or dangerous situations on the way to the airport. Thankfully the fifteen-minute drive to the airport was seamless. We found out later that the next day the road was completely blocked by protestors for the next week. Cars were blocked and set on fire, and police officers were beaten on the highway to the airport. The Lord had brought us out in His timing, but the relief was outweighed by uncertainty of what lay ahead.

Redding was beautiful. During crisis, God actually started an amazing work in the hearts of my two oldest children there. Bethany describes it as a turnaround moment for her when she truly began to follow the Lord and love Him with all her heart, and Ethan received a prophetic word that is still framed beside his bed. Surprisingly, in the healing rooms where we had hoped God would heal Nathan's kidneys, He healed me. All the neurological symptoms and leg pain that had tortured me for the last several months were gone. We were refreshed, changed, and brought into such a place of peace that it could have only come from our Creator.

THE CONFIRMATION

A few days later, we stepped back into Nathan's old doctor's office in North Carolina. While waiting to see the doctor I was thinking about how we would tell him our story and how this all transpired. I believed that he would say either that Nathan was miraculously healed after looking at his new lab work or that his condition wasn't too serious and that the nephrologist in Honduras was overreacting. What I was not prepared for was the confirmation that Nathan needed to start dialysis immediately to save his life. I felt anger and indignation rise within me while he spoke. "What about our children?" I asked. "We can't stay here!" He said there was no other choice and that this was to protect Nathan's life. At that moment, I knew our lives were about to change drastically, and I knew I was about to step into something that would prove to be the hardest season of our lives. And it was.

HARD DECISIONS

Then began the slew of hard decisions that had to be made over the next couple of weeks, while attempting to divert the stress away from our oldest children, who were also celebrating the first Christmas with their extended family for the first time in several years. We now knew that until God healed Nathan, he would have to remain in North Carolina and prepare for dialysis. The doctor didn't even want him to travel back to tell his children goodbye and pack some more of his belongings. He would be there indefinitely. I prayed and felt that we were to give our oldest children, Ethan and Bethany, the choice to stay in North Carolina or to return with me to Honduras, which was still in political upheaval. Nathan agreed, and so when we gave Ethan and Bethany the choice, they both chose to stay in North Carolina with Nathan and our families. Despite my longing as a mother to have them with me, I knew that they heard from the Lord, and I felt peace in their decision to stay.

I knew I would have to return to Honduras soon. I left Gabriel and Camila under the care of my good friend and fellow missionary, Nancy, but she could not care for them long term, and my heart ached to go back to them. It was then that we were presented, by others around us at the time, with another option that seemed like wisdom. It was the option to forfeit our adoptions of the children that we had cared for most of their lives, all move permanently to North Carolina, and allow the children's authority in Honduras to find new homes for our children. This option was thrust at us more than once and came from people that we loved and held in high regard in our lives. Our devastating situation became harder as we lacked support, and we were uncertain about the future of our whole family.

It was at that time that I cried out to God for a word, a revelation that would sustain us through whatever decision we made, and He answered me. Although I wanted to hear a thunderous voice from Heaven that told me exactly what I was to do, His reply was quite different, but just as powerful.

Through His whisper He spoke,
"If you choose the hard path, I will bless you more
than you can imagine."

It was settled at that moment. I spoke with Nathan, and we came into agreement. We would fight not only for Nathan's life, but for all our children, and we trusted that God would care for us and be faithful to His word.

Journal Entry, January 3, 2018

Father, I feel somewhat numb. Trying to push through to see the greater work and experience all that You have for me during this time. I pray that You awaken my spirit and help me to stay firm. I feel like a fog surrounds me...like an alternate reality surrounds me, unable to fully push through to the reality that is You. I know in my heart that You are doing a great work. You are keeping your promises and working all of this to the good of those who love You. Help me Father to stay true to You. Your will, Your way. Now is the time to show in the natural that I truly believe all that I have confessed. I need more of You. I need to experience You and Your grace. I come confidently before the throne of grace to obtain mercy. That You would pour out tangible truths today to remind me of Your love and promises for me and my family. You are my Father, my Daddy, and I am so grateful for Your love. However, Father, I need affirmation from You today. You have taught me to not seek it from man, but I need it from You today. Affirm that we are on the right path, that we continue to be led by your Holy Spirit and that you are doing a greater work. Help my faith to arise today to cling to Your robe, Your promises. I refuse to partner with the enemy and any of his lies today. I hold to your promises, even if I can't see them being fulfilled in this moment. I cling to You, my Hope. I miss my children, Father. I know that You above

*all understand. Reunite me with them and soothe my heart.
Bring my husband into full health and restore his youth.
Restore our family from the tear of two countries. You alone
I can trust. You are my only hope, and You are faithful.
Amen.*

Journal Entry, January 15, 2018

*"Because you have chosen the harder road in the name of
Love, I will give you what you seek. I will give you the
desires of your heart and open doors that no man can close."*

*I choose Gabriel and Camila, Father. I choose the harder
thing and your blessings that come with it.*

*Father says, "You will tame wild hearts and burst open
rivers in dry places through my Spirit."*

*He is preparing us for the season we are now in. All of this
is temporary affliction, but it will work together for our
good and His glory. Many are the afflictions of the
righteous, but the Lord delivers them out of them ALL.
Nathan's healing is complete in Jesus' name. He has poured
out abundant love within us with the ability to push in for
the ones that the world will not. It is a testimony to the
love that He has poured out in us and the way He fights for*

each of us. Our life is a demonstration like that of Ezekiel, and in faithfulness we will see the rewards and fruit.

Journal Entry, January 16, 2018

The Lord says, "I am releasing a new wind upon the earth that contains a love and passion like never before and those who genuinely love Me and seek Me will carry this new wind with them and experience the outpouring of my Spirit like never before. It will invade communities, cities, and the nations. Where wisdom and knowledge led hearts to me, now a love and passion for Me will. It will be combined with a pureness and a burning away of old things and new life will spring forth."

"I pray that out of His glorious riches He may strengthen you with power through His Spirit in your inner being, so that Christ may dwell in your hearts through faith. And I pray that you, being rooted and established in love, may have power, together with all the Lord's holy people, to grasp how wide and long and high and deep is the love of Christ, and to know this love that surpasses knowledge — that you may be filled to the measure of all the fullness of God." Ephesians 3:16-19 (NIV)

THE HARD ROAD

GABRIEL

The hard path was harder than I could have ever realized. I found myself often daydreaming and reminding myself of the miraculous story of my children, and how I fought for them. Each of my children are a testimony to the goodness of God, and they all have their own stories.

When we arrived in Honduras in 2014, we were in the last stages of a failed Ethiopian adoption. In 2013, we received the referral of a little boy whom we named Elias. We were preparing for travel to meet him when our adoption agency at the time was convicted of adoption fraud. Although we had done nothing illegal, we never received communication regarding Elias again. It was a devastating blow emotionally and financially. So, although we felt led to adopt, we were not ready to start another venture, especially in a new country, but God had other plans. After connecting with a local missionary we were blindsided with the proposal to foster; however, surprisingly after praying, we felt good to move forward. Things moved faster than we had anticipated, and the next day workers from children's services were at our house to do a home study. Because of all the adoption paperwork we had from the previous adoption, we were amazingly prepared, and on September 29, 2014, we were called to come and pick up our son.

We drove on the long gravel road past the juvenile prison on the outskirts of town to an orphanage called *Nueva Esperanza* (Spanish for New Hope). As we waited inside the cement building, we noticed another family we had met the day before for the first time — the Boyle family. Todd Boyle and his wife Wendy had also decided to foster, and on that day, they took home two girls including Camila, whose story would ultimately intertwine with ours in the months to come. I watched as the workers brought the children out to Todd and Wendy and saw them lovingly embrace the girls. It was after that when a woman came in holding a baby boy in a brown onesie three sizes too big, wrapped in a towel with holes in it and holding a bottle. She handed him to me, and my heart immediately was overwhelmed with emotions. We signed two papers, and that was it. We left that day as a family of five, and although everyone had said it was only fostering, not adoption, I knew that this boy named Gabriel was a part of me, and I felt the love of my Father.

CHANGING COURSE

We knew early on in our fostering of Gabriel and Camila that we wanted to be their forever family. I often imagined what that would look like when they were infants and how we would someday be able to come and go as a family without the legal constraints. I imagined their futures, and I imagined them always calling me mom. We started the process of adoption when they were two years old. We were told by the government that we could adopt and that the adoptions would be completed within six months. We planned to adopt as Honduran residents, not US citizens, which meant they could not immigrate immediately to the US (per US law), but we were excited. That excitement weaned as the six months came and went and their promise unfulfilled. We were told we had to complete three years of residency to move forward, and so we waited.

Through prayer, we discerned that we were fighting an anti-adoption spirit in the nation and that there were spiritual powers that did not want our children to be released into their destinies. Almost to the date of obtaining our three years of residency Nathan moved back to North Carolina. At that point we could no longer adopt as residents, and the adoptions were changed to international. A large portion of my time visiting the US the first several months of 2018 consisted of home studies, getting fingerprints, meeting with notaries, and preparing for their hopeful arrival. Our adoption agency had compassion on our situation and thought we were the best fit for the children, but they realistically relayed to us that our chances were slim at best. Honduran law required that both parents be in a healthy physical state and expected to sustain throughout the children's youth; additionally, two unrelated siblings could not be adopted within two years of each other. Ultimately, they were required to do what was in the best interest of each child, which we had going for us, but it would still take a God-sized miracle.

ALL ALONE

Although I was surrounded by people most of the time in Honduras, I often felt all alone. Living as a single mother in a country that was not my own, in a culture that was not my own, proved to be the loneliest experience of my life. I expected my friends and fellow missionaries to understand the gaping hole in my heart and to come in and fill it. The more I longed for someone or something besides the Lord, the more He withdrew them from me. I was confused. I was angry and bitter, and then the Lord began to whisper to my heart once again. "Look to Me," He said. I had tried to fill God's place with other people. I wanted someone to lift us out of this pit. Someone to do the work that only God could do. But I heard Him, and I knew He was right. My perspective changed and my mindset shifted as I realized I would need to go back to my first love for comfort during this time, and when I did, forgiveness flooded my heart. For two weeks I poured out my heart to Him, asking for forgiveness for carrying offense toward those who I expected to fill His place, toward those who went on with life as usual while mine was falling apart, toward those who chose not to comfort me during my hardest time. Tears of repentance and love flowed as I wept often while in the shower, while driving, while folding clothes. The Lord was preparing me for the battle, not with flesh and blood, but with the principalities of darkness, and I had to let go of the enemy's weapons in order to pick up those of the Lord.

Journal Entry, February 20, 2018

To love deeply and truly as Christ, there is a vulnerability that is full of risks. The risk of losing, your love not being reciprocated, hurt, but the love that our Father has called us to goes beyond hurt, offense, unmet expectations, loss, grief. It is our greatest power, yet often our greatest weakness. He is calling us deeper into a passionate love relationship with Him that radiates out of us to our friends, family, enemies. May we be known by our most precious fruit: love.

SHE WILL BRING YOU JOY

When our mission's agency asked how long we thought the process would last and I would be going back and forth from Honduras to the United States, I consulted our dear friend and trusted lawyer. "Eight months," she replied. If all went according to plan, we would be bringing our children home by August 2018. "Ok, I can do this," I thought. I was so focused on finishing the race, even though every day that passed felt like an eternity and another tear in my heart. I wanted to believe it would be done quickly, in part because I didn't want to fathom the alternative, even though as was often the case in Honduras, or in life, things rarely go according to plan. However, this trial and affliction would change the destiny of our children, set a foundation for their future generations, and bring glory to God.

I knew that God would go before us, for I had already seen how He had written the miraculous story of Gabriel and Camila and woven them together with such love that no man could deny His hand. The first few months of fostering Gabriel were busy as Nathan and I started caring for him in the middle of serving in a ten-week missionary internship, but that didn't stop us. He was right in the middle of ministry and all that we did, alongside Ethan and Bethany. He was such a blessing and brought fullness to our family; yet, in 2012 God had spoken to our hearts that we would adopt not one but two children, both at once. When we got the referral for our Ethiopian son, I thought I had missed that word from the Lord, but it turns out I didn't. Three months after Gabriel came into our family, we were sharing New Year's Eve with the Boyle Family, whom we had met at the orphanage. We had started to form a special bond with them around our love for the Lord and the children that He had entrusted to us. They had since that time fostered several other children along with Camila, who was six months old at the time.

That evening Camila spent a good portion of the time snuggled in Nathan's arms. They bonded instantly. Wendy approached me as they were leaving that night. She had known that our hearts were to care for another child at some point and, as we were near the doorway, made a comment that swelled my heart. "Maybe Camila is meant for your family," she said with a slight smile. My heart pondered this as Nathan, and I prayed throughout the next week on this life-changing decision. Looking for a definitive answer, I smiled as I heard the Lord say, "She will bring you joy." On February 6, 2015, we welcomed Camila, our joy, into our home.

Camila and Gabriel, although not related by birth, had miraculously entered the same orphanage on the same day, slept next to each other in the same crib at the orphanage, left the orphanage on the same day to be fostered, and now were reunited in the same home. No man could have coordinated with such detail and accuracy what God had planned for these two children, and I knew that their stories would not end in despair.

HELP HAS ARRIVED

I was back in Honduras when Nathan was sent to the hospital to receive his dialysis catheter. This was it. It was really going to happen. I longed to be there with him as he began this journey to fight for his life, but I couldn't. I was in Honduras, praying and seeking God for someone to stand alongside our family long term during our most difficult season and care for Gabriel and Camila so I could go to the United States. I constantly pushed back fear and anxiety, and for a time I had to bury all my emotions so I could function in the moment. I allowed myself to cry every morning, in the shower. I would pray and ask God to deliver us, giving Him all I had in that moment. I would then dry my face, get dressed and focus on the task ahead. It was the only way that I could cope. But I still wondered who would care for my children, my most valuable treasures, and love them like their own. Who would sacrifice so much for our family? It was something I could hardly think to ask anyone during normal circumstances. But these weren't normal circumstances, and I needed help for the sake of my children's future.

It wasn't long before the Lord sent His divine help through the family that would run this race with us, and it wasn't who I expected. Wendy told me that their family not only wanted to walk alongside during this time but felt it was their calling. I cried tears of relief but also sadness that this was the reality. For both of our families. Yet God had made a way when there was no other way, and He removed the mountain in front of us so that we could continue on our path. So, for the next ten months, Wendy, who at this point lived four hours from San Pedro, traveled every month or two, to my home to care for my children. She left her own husband and seven children to care for my children for weeks at a time, and she never once expressed regret or anger in her decision to care for my children or how my family took away from her own family. What we were doing seemed foolish to the world: believing in God to do the impossible in a broken system and risking our families, safety, and hearts to do what we thought was right in the Lord. There are times when I wondered about the outcome, but I had to give it all to God. I was in too deep. I had to just keep moving forward.

REALITY SANK IN

The doctors finally decided on a date to insert Nathan's dialysis catheter. Despite our believing for his kidneys to be miraculously healed, Nathan was checked in the hospital for same day surgery. His father took my place by his side and a routine procedure to insert an eight-inch tube into his abdomen turned into a couple nights stay in the hospital and several pints of blood given. It felt at the time that every bit of grace that had sustained Nathan for fourteen years had been lifted, but in reality, there was an enemy roaming around like a lion, seeking whom he may devour. Despite his best attempts, the grace and protection did remain on Nathan. After Nathan had healed for a couple weeks, I returned to North Carolina, and we found ourselves in the dialysis clinic for training. We were given a fifty-pound machine that would be Nathan's natural lifeline and do what his kidneys could not, which was to filter out the toxins from his body. We sat through teaching, surrounded by patients almost twice Nathan's age, trying to soak in all the dos and don'ts of peritoneal dialysis. That night we gloved up, masked up, read through all the instructions, and hooked my husband up to machine that would filter his blood over the next eight hours while he slept. In time, the loud humming of the machine was a comfort for me as I laid next to my husband at night. It reminded me that there was something at work bringing life to my husband, and there was also Someone doing the same. And for that, I was grateful.

FINISHING THE WORK

Nathan and I had spent the last several years pouring our lives into the Honduran people and our team of missionaries. Although we would be down one, I realized the work that we started as team leaders and apprenticeship directors needed to be completed. When

I traveled back in January, there were three months left for two families and a single in their apprenticeship. For two years, they had worked diligently, and we needed to press hard to accomplish what God had begun. I found that my teachings changed, my perspective shifted, and my devotions that previously focused on the love and grace of God now focused on endurance, perseverance and doing the hard things, the only thing I could teach on during this crisis. I was teaching them as much as I was teaching myself, but it was then that *I realized there are some things that cannot be taught by teaching. They have to be taught through experience. While I was in the middle of being broken, they were enduring towards their mark, the race that had been set before them. Even in my brokenness, I was called to be faithful in what God had set before me. I held tightly to the faith that after the breaking would come a putting back together by His hands that would make me stronger than before.*

In the months following I was able to finish what I had started for our missionaries with the help of the Lord. The banquet that I had organized for the apprentices was modest. I've never been much of a party planner, and my overly practical ways sometimes do not always lead to beautiful displays, but my heart was full. I had watched them overcome the odds and successfully cross their finish lines. They would now be moving into greater authority and leadership in their callings as missionaries. One couple would go on to direct a bible school that is equipping Hondurans, who are in turn ministering to their communities. The other couple went on to direct a farming project that transformed a whole community in rural Honduras. Our last apprentice went on to teach carpentry and other career skills to high-risk youth. In that moment, I felt a sense of accomplishment, and it was a boost for me to see them cross their finish line, even when I was still running mine.

Journal Entry, May 12, 2018

Father, I love You. I need You now more than ever, and my heart yearns for You more than my next breath. There is something deep within me pulling me closer and deeper in You. Help me not to resist it or deny it, for it is life. Forgive me Father for my lack, my sins, my complacency and thank You for your forgiveness. Thank You for seeing me in my fullness and drawing me into that fullness. I praise You and thank You for your immeasurable goodness and love for me. Thank You for opening the doors that no man can close. Thank You for growing faith that will release Your immense power, that will be demonstrated through me, not because of me, but always because of You. In my weakness You are made strong, and your power can flow. Less of me and more of You, Father. Come Holy Spirit and guide me in every moment. Pour out immense love and wisdom on how to use it. I bind every work of the enemy in our lives today and declare faith will arise even greater today and align with your grace to produce miracles. Adoptions done. Healing for all our family done. Thousands upon thousands knowing you done. Disciples made in Jesus' name. Today is the day of salvation. I will rejoice and be glad in it. Praise You my good and gracious Father. I love You. Amen.

CALL TO PERSEVERE

———————

ALL MY CHILDREN

As long as I have been a mother, I have been one to stay near my children most of the time. I always enjoyed their presence, their unique personalities, and the security that came with keeping them close. The occasional sleepover with wonderful grandparents even came with a bit of a strain as I struggled to let them wonder far. So, it was this area that hit me the hardest during that time. I had stood in faith for well over a decade believing for life and healing for Nathan but learning to trust God to be the protector of my children's hearts, minds, bodies and emotions took a whole new level of trust. I felt that I didn't have enough preparation for this change, but it was thrust upon me quickly. I had spent most of my motherhood seemingly trying to do all that I could to protect them and keep them from harm, but now, no matter what decision I made there would be consequences. I couldn't keep them from all the trauma that was unfolding in the battle, and I was constantly making hard decisions. I felt the immense loss while continually trying to look forward to the future because the present was too hard.

After six months, during their summer vacation, I finally had all four of my children under the same roof in Honduras. I was overcome with feelings of relief and peace, but that summer it was often combined with heavy emotions as all four of my children were in the middle of transition while not knowing exactly where they were transitioning. I wanted to give them answers and certainly, but all I had was faith. At last, I had all my children together, but I felt that I was failing each of them, and I didn't know when we would find ourselves on dry land again.

Journal Entry, September 18, 2018

My most beautiful and gracious Father, one year since I began journaling and writing the words that You laid on my heart. A year since the flood of the Holy Spirit that penetrated me deeply for a season, although I know Your presence still remains. My body and emotions are tired this morning, like previous mornings, but my spirit is strong and steadfast in Your promises. My mind renewed and taking captive the thoughts of the great enemy. I do ask for a renewing of my soul today, Father, that my emotions will not betray me and lead me into sin today. That I will be led by the Spirit alone. That my soul and the many losses be healed in Jesus' name. Amen.

A TURNAROUND DAY

August came and went without the adoptions being completed. In fact, the first part of the process, which was finalizing their abandonment decrees, hadn't even been completed. I was tired, and the energy that had sustained me for the first year of crisis was leaving. The energy that I had for finishing apprenticeships, cultivating relationships, and doing ministry outreach was weaning, and so was my energy for single-parenting two toddlers. Months without their father, siblings, and sometimes mother started catching up with my children. Emotions that were once kept in balance were now in crisis mode.

It was November and rainy season in Honduras. It wasn't far from Thanksgiving, although that would be another holiday that our family would not spend together. The day before had started out well, but as usual in that season, had ended in tears and frustration. I called Wendy in desperation after my then four-year-old son Gabriel had cornered me in his room, yelling at me and hitting me, while his sister, Camila, jeered him on and laughed. I was devastated. The very children for whom I was fighting for were hurting me. The reality is they were hurting too, and angry, and they needed a mother who made them feel secure. They needed a mother who would hold them accountable and hold a firm line in which they could find safety. I carried so much guilt for not being able to give each of my children and husband what they deserved. They all deserved all of me, but there was just one me. Realistically, I couldn't do it all, and that left me in a place of regret as deep as the ocean. That is when I cried out to the Lord, and He answered me. He spoke to me, saying, "You have given your children grace, but yourself, not enough." Those words changed my life that day, and I realized I could no longer carry the same guilt and allow my life to be disregarded. It was not the same thing; I still had value.

The next day, I woke up in prayer. I knew that if there was going to be change, it would have to be now. The day went well through breakfast until about mid-morning when we three marched upstairs to get ready for the day. I wanted to get the children ready so I could get a quick shower, but Gabriel had other plans. He did not want to brush his teeth, and my asking him to do so started an erratic chain reaction of verbal assault. I felt the Lord's grace over me, the very thing I was aspiring to understand, that allowed me to do what He had called me to do that day. In that moment, I emotionally detached from Gabriel and stood my ground, asking that he please brush his teeth. After further angry outbursts,

I told him to take some time on his bed to reset and that we would try again later. Then began the hitting and the anger. Whereas the day before I had been pinned in a corner, that day I folded my arms around him (as not to hurt him) and pinned him for the next ten minutes. During that time, he raged. He yelled out for help in one moment, followed by laughter in the next, and angry insults the next. I did not say a word as I held his tense body. Finally, after ten minutes, his body went limp, and he very calmly said, "I'm done."

That moment changed both our lives and my parenting. It was then when I realized that the next season of my life would not only be spent warring to reunite our family and for my husband to live but also to be the mother my children needed, while extending grace to myself. What my united family required during the last season was not the same as my separated family needed now, and I would have to learn from the Lord how to parent differently. It would begin a whole new breaking within me. I wasn't sure if it would break me past what I could handle, but I knew that it had to be done, and I knew that God would have to help me.

MOVING DAY

Over the next several weeks, our family saw drastic
changes, and the Lord was honoring the work of my
hands and heart. Gabriel, although quick to anger at
times, never attempted to hit me again. He was more
confident, secure, and loving. Camila, who had
previously withheld love from me, started to let me kiss
her again and receive my affection. We were making
strides, and then we began another major transition.
Wendy had traveled all year long to help our family, and
it was now time for us to move to her. It was time. She
lived in the capital of Honduras, where our adoptions
would need to be completed. We had been living in the
same neighborhood in San Pedro Sula since arriving in
Honduras, and although my husband no longer lived
there with me, it was hard letting go. It provided some
sense of security in my time of uncertainty, but I knew it
was time to let go. Our missionary team arrived early in
the morning to help pack the moving van that would go
ahead of us for the four-hour trek. The landlord came to
get the keys from me as the kids and I said goodbye to
our home and our missionary community. My heart was
heavy as I drove out of town, knowing that this would
no longer be my home, but I was ready for completion,
for the next step, and this was it. Nancy, who had cared

for my children earlier in the year, had graciously offered to accompany me on the trip, and I eagerly accepted her companionship.

The trip around the mountains and lakes of Honduras took a toll on the children. After stopping several times from the children crying, vomiting, using the restroom, and begging to get out of their car seats, we arrived at the property. However, relief turned to feelings of being overwhelmed as the moving truck got stuck at the gate and could not enter our driveway. It was at a standstill with all our belongings nearly a tenth of a mile from our home, and the sun was already setting. Quickly, a new neighbor and friend responded to the need. We spent the next few hours unloading our belongings into the road and back into our cars to be delivered to our home.

Although exhausted, we were there. It was an old ranch house in the mountains of Honduras. It was not what we were used to, but it was less than a third of the price we were paying in San Pedro, and after a year of living in two countries and multiple plane trips, we were falling into debt fast. Also, it was on the land next to Todd and Wendy, which would be helpful in the coming months.

MOVEMENT AT LAST

With only days to spare before the whole government of Honduras closed for their month-long Christmas vacation, I finally received a date for Camila's abandonment hearing. Before the kids' official adoption procedures could move forward, they both had to be legally declared abandoned. This meant extensive searches for birth parents, relatives, and hospital records by the two social workers responsible for all adoption cases in a region of close to a million people. After months of home visits, psychological testing, and multiple visits to DINAF (Honduras' children's welfare agency), Camila and I walked into the courthouse. I was expecting something of grandeur, but the room that we walked into was simple, and the judge wore regular clothes. It was then that they asked Camila to go into another room with the psychologist while I attended the proceeding. I sat in a chair as half a dozen people had all eyes on me. They read the official case in Spanish, and although I had spent nearly the last decade of my life learning Spanish, the courtroom language, coupled with my racing heart, seemed to take away my understanding. After several minutes, they finished, and the court lawyer asked if there was anything I would like to add. There was so much to say, so much I could explain. I wanted to tell them just how much I loved her and how I had fought for her, but the only words I could get out were, "I love her, and I just want the best for her."

I wage war in the name of Jesus against the enemy and his demons that are attacking families, the fatherless, the government and God's chosen ones in the nation of Honduras. I declare that I will no longer stay quiet or unaware to the schemes of the evil one to bring destruction. I break and demolish every argument and claim that sets itself up against the knowledge of God. I take captive every thought of every government worker, every DINAF worker, every lawyer, every psychologist, every foster or adoptive family, and every person working in children's rights in Honduras, and declare they must be obedient to Christ. I break the strongholds of fatherlessness, trauma, pride, death, complacency, control, and python spirit, in the name of Jesus. I break all agreements with the enemy and declare that DINAF and the government of Honduras no longer have the authority to make decisions for God's children based on the enemy's lies or influence in Jesus' name. I declare the scales are removed from their eyes and that their minds are renewed by the knowledge and wisdom of Christ. We take all power, authority and dominion and declare that justice will reign, and that the fatherless will be adopted into the families that God has appointed. I declare the knowledge, wisdom and heart of God will prevail in all situations and future decisions. I declare an open heaven over every child waiting for a family and that the enemy no longer has the right to block them from their appointed families and destiny in Christ. I declare salvation to all DINAF and government workers and a supernatural upheaval in the spirit that leads to a change in the natural. I declare freedom in Christ and a breaking away from every generational curse over Honduras and a season of new beginnings in Christ. I declare the enemy may not linger or draw out this process, but that by the declarations and prayers of the righteous, based on the authority that Christ has given us, that it will happen quickly in the name of Jesus, and as these things come to pass it will serve as a testimony for all time to the glory, power, and goodness of our wonderful Father. Amen!

I declare that even as our family's story is brought upon the workers at DINAF that they are overcome with such compassion, love and understanding that they are brought to their knees. That it will be a personal pursuit to bring our children into our family. That even as the words leave their lips that it will bring a revival among the workers at DINAF that will spread across the country and usher in change and children into families. That we will experience such favor and grace with DINAF that even those around them will be shocked, but they will have the mind and heart of Christ. It will be a testimony that no man can boast in, but that God will receive all glory and honor for generations. Revival of hearts and passion to see children in families righteous will be exalted in the land and given extreme favor. All plans of the enemy are broken in Jesus' name, all attempts to foil God's plans to cause trauma and to confuse are broken in Jesus' name and healing and restoration come swiftly in Jesus' name. Amen!

NEEDED GRACE

SECOND CHRISTMAS APART

It was difficult to accept the fact that one year had come and gone with our family separated and that we would be spending yet another Christmas apart. I decided to celebrate Christmas early with Gabriel and Camila since I had missed their Christmas the year before. It was about a week before Christmas, and I prepared them the night before that we would wake up and celebrate the next day. I woke up early and wheeled in their new bikes into the cold living room. The mountains of Honduras were drastically cooler than what we were used to feeling in San Pedro Sula, and 50° felt frigid on our drafty house's cold tile floors without central air or heating. After starting my coffee, the kids came running out from their bed. It was a new day, and their smiles were priceless. They were so excited. Because of the cold outside, I let them ride their bikes in our old ranch house all day long. It was a good day.

The next day, with my bags packed again, I listened to them tell me that they didn't want me to go, like every time before. I cried for the majority of the next two hours as I drove half the way to San Pedro Sula, stopping to spend the night at a fellow missionary's home. There was a missionary family there who was struggling with family and heart issues, and although I wasn't sure what I could possibly give, I offered to meet with them. I spent the next several hours ministering to deep hurts, regrets, and offense. I watched as the Lord healed an entire family—not me, but Him, and within a few hours their family was changed. I received a note months later that gave glory to God for what He had done that day, and I knew that one day that would be me. I believed one day after it was all over, He would release healing upon our family.

The next day, I made the flights back to North Carolina, and I felt the love in our tight embraces. I wanted to make all the times together count, trying to make up for lost time. We bonded over movies and favorite foods, and we talked about how our lives would eventually turn out. Nathan even saved the Christmas decorations so I could put them up with Ethan and Bethany. I soaked up every minute with them that Christmas, fully aware that it would soon be time to leave again. I enjoyed Christmas the best I could, knowing that the disappointment was real. We were not together, but we tried to set our eyes on the hope that was before us.

Our families mourned our losses, and yet I struggled to find anyone that could relate to where I was. I could not even fully relate to where I was. I realized that I stopped unpacking my bags every time I travelled back and forth. I stopped making unnecessary trips out. I craved rest. I wanted to hold tight to my family and not let go. I wanted what I couldn't have in that season and longed for more, but through my distress, I mustered up more longing to draw closer to the Lord.

Journal Entry, January 14, 2019

"Whenever our hearts make us feel guilty and remind us of our failures, we know that God is much greater and more merciful than our conscience, and he knows everything there is to know about us. My delightfully loved friends, when our hearts don't condemn us, we have a bold freedom to speak face-to-face with God. And whatever we ask of him we receive because we keep his commands. And by our beautiful intentions we continue to do what brings pleasure to him. So, these are his commands: that we continually place our trust in the name of his Son, Jesus Christ, and that we keep loving one another, just as he has commanded us. For all who obey his commands find their lives joined in union with him, and he lives and flourishes in them. We

know and have proof that he constantly lives and flourishes in us, by the Spirit that he has given us."
1 John 3:20-24 (TPT)

Father,
Forgive me for underestimating your love and grace. You are the most amazing Father, and I am so proud to be Yours. I am Yours and You are mine. You are my greatest joy and reward. Thank You for loving me. Thank You for Your patience and grace. Continue to cleanse my heart. Draw me closer to You, my Father. May my life be a continual life union with You. May I love like You, live like You, forgive like You, and bring healing like You. Holy Spirit may I let You lead in all situations of my life. I choose You. Your will. Your way. I praise You Holy Spirit and thank You for dwelling in me. May You flourish more and more each day within me. As I follow You and go deeper in Your will and love, I ask that You bring closure and justice to this season of our lives. That the enemy is not allowed to prolong what You have for each of us. I declare destinies fulfilled, healing activated and fulfilled, grace and favor released, destines realized and love unfathomable actualized. This is what I ask for in the name of your precious and powerful son, Jesus. Praise be forever to your wonderful name, Father. I love You and wait in anticipation and faith for what You are doing. Amen!

Journal Entry, January 23, 2019

"Don't be pulled in different directions or worried about a thing. Be saturated in prayer throughout each day, offering your faith-filled requests before God with overflowing gratitude. Tell him every detail of your life, then God's wonderful peace that transcends human understanding, will make the answers known to you through Jesus Christ. Keep your thoughts continually fixed on all that is authentic and real, honorable, and admirable, beautiful and respectful, pure and holy, merciful and kind. And fasten your thoughts on every glorious work of God, praising him always." Philippians 4:6-8 (TPT)

Father,
I praise You and bless You today in my tiredness. I choose to not worry, but instead bring my petitions to You today with gratitude. Father, I grow weary from this season. My heart yearns for reunification, restitution, healing in my family. I am so grateful for everything You have blessed us with in this season, most of all You. That will always be enough. However, I long for justice and closing of a season. My heart yearns to be with Nathan in my homeland and for our children to be with us. For Nathan to be healed. Please Lord bring your justice, your love and resolution. Hope deferred makes a heart sick, and I feel sick this morning. Sick with grief and my body is tired and bears the burden

of hard emotions. Please heal me Father and bring Your Spirit and justice. I ask this in the precious name of Jesus Christ. Amen.

BETHANY

My daughter Bethany was eleven by this time. She has always been such a joy to me, and everyone calls her my "mini-me". She is strong, brave, thoughtful, and fun. She was only two years old when we were called into full time missions and had grown up on the mission field in Central America. I never imagined that I would not be with her as she transitioned back into her own culture. God's grace covered her, but this trial was difficult for her. Although she had been safe with her father in North Carolina, I sensed it was time for her to come back with me to Honduras for this return trip. She and Ethan had spent the previous summer with me and the children in Honduras, but this would be her first time in our new home. A lot had changed in a year, but thankfully, God was changing all of us as well, including Bethany.

Gabriel and Camila were so excited to see their sister, and she enjoyed witnessing their new milestones. They constantly called her name to show her their next new trick. She and the Boyle girls got to record each other in their homemade mystery films, and Gabriel and Camila constantly interrupted their work, eager to spend time with her. I dearly missed Ethan and Nathan, but Bethany being with me brought me so much comfort. During the mornings after, I would wake earlier than any of them and watch them as they slept, thanking God for each of them, yet at the same time crying out for deliverance. My heart felt more whole, but the next few months came with extreme challenges. Our family was nearing the point of possible adoption referral, and I did not expect any of the challenges that followed.

COUNTERATTACKS

While we were gaining ground, the enemy started his counterattacks, and they were fierce. They started with the ticks. After returning from the US over Christmas, my pet-free home was overrun with ticks. These ticks were not like the ticks normal in the US, but rather they were pin sized ticks, smaller than the size of a freckle. Although they didn't cause apparent harm to Bethany or me, it quickly became apparent that Gabriel and Camila's immune systems were not handling the bites well. It started with a bite here and there that then began multiplying. I started keeping the kids indoors to avoid the large weeds outside where the ticks congregated. I had the house fumigated. We got sprays, oils, creams, and bracelets. I even tried getting the kid's pajamas directly from the dryer every night so that the ticks wouldn't sneak into the clothes. It was all to no avail.

One morning in late January, I woke up to find almost a hundred bites covering Gabriel and a handful on Camila's stomach. I was terrified, and at the time I didn't realize it was the ticks because I didn't see them. I decided to take the children to San Pedro Sula to see one of my friends who was a medical doctor. Bethany, Gabriel, Camila, and I traveled several hours driving to find solutions. After consulting my friend who was a pediatrician, I did not have an answer, so I decided to go to one of the best dermatologists in Honduras. After he checked Gabriel, the doctor concluded that he had an overreactive immune response to the tick bites and that his body produced dozens and dozens of "mimic bites" in response that were larger than the actual bites. The doctor said he hadn't seen a case that severe, and never with a mother that cared for her children the way I did. I knew it was an attack from the enemy, and it had brought in fear.

At that moment I decided to take a trip to the beach two hours away from San Pedro Sula with my three children to let the salt water heal the children's skin and the Lord restore my soul. When we reached our destination, we stayed two nights and I was refreshed as I allowed the Lord once again heal me. The vastness of the ocean helped me to come up to a higher perspective and remember God's promises as I deeply breathed in the fresh air. After our visit, we traveled back to San Pedro, anticipating our departure the next day to join a four-day missionary retreat that my daughter was very much looking forward to joining. That is when I got a call from Nathan that they had found a donor.

Once Nathan was on dialysis for six months, he could then apply to the waiting list for a kidney transplant. It would be a kidney from an expired donor (someone who passed away and wanted to donate their kidney). He was listed on two different waiting lists, and the average waiting time was five years. However, Nathan had gotten a call two weeks prior and was told that he was on standby because he was next on the list to receive a kidney. I remember feeling guilty and indignant about Nathan receiving a kidney. It was a blessing after all, but I still held on to the hope of miraculous healing, and in part, I just couldn't stand the thought of more difficulty.

I got the call upstairs at our ministry center in San Pedro. Nathan said that he had just gotten selected, and surgery would be the next afternoon. It was midday, and I was faced with the reality of coordinating the Boyles to care for my children (who were at this point four hours away), book a flight that could make it to Nathan on time, pack, and get to the airport. As I hung up the phone, I felt sick. This was supposed to be a happy moment, but I felt dread. After booking the only flight that would make it to Nathan's surgery in time, I met the Boyles halfway to their home, I kissed Gabriel and Camila goodbye once again, and Bethany and I set off for the airport.

Our flight was flying late at night and would have us traveling through multiple cities, but at least we would make it to Nathan and see him before his surgery. Before we left San Pedro, the warfare began. Bethany and I were selected by the airline for "inspection". We were escorted by several armed, male security officers out of the airport during the dark night and into a room beneath the airport where they searched all our bags and asked us multiple questions. I have had many similarly risky situations over the years, situations in which I felt peace, but this night, I felt violated and angry. I held my tongue as I prayed for the Lord to protect Bethany and me. He did, and we were soon sent back, the last to board the plane.

We arrived at New York in a new airport during the early morning hours, and then Nathan called and said that his surgery had been moved up. He would now be going back to surgery at 6:30am. My heart sank, and I felt the air being punched out of my lungs. I wouldn't be able to reach him in time to see him before his surgery, and there was nothing I could do. Then, while Bethany and I were flying from New York to North Carolina, I got a message from my sister-in-law. It said "Call me. It's an emergency." I couldn't call. I was in the air, and we wouldn't land for an hour. She tried to call me, and my phone died. I immediately went to plug in my cellphone, and I realized we were flying a new plane carrier that did not have electrical outlets. At that moment, I did not know if Nathan was alive or dead. I did not know what I would discover coming home. All I knew was that I needed to pray.

BACKED INTO A CORNER

Heather, my friend and sister-in-Christ of nearly two decades, picked Bethany and me up at the airport, and we both sat in silence with tears running down our faces as we headed to the hospital. It was the same hospital where I had given birth to Ethan and Bethany and had worked as a nursing assistant during nursing school. I had good memories from there, but this day my heart sank as we drove near.

We were almost there when I was able to speak with my sister-in-law on the phone. She told me that Nathan was alive, but something went wrong during the surgery. I was so grateful in that moment to know that he was alive, and any worries and anxiety I was experiencing paled in comparison to the relief I felt that moment. I walked to the waiting room where one of the surgeons was waiting for me. He explained that while they were preparing Nathan for surgery, the large bore tube that they inserted into his neck had perforated through the vein, and Nathan had bled significantly into and around his lungs. They didn't catch it until his blood pressure started dropping; by the time they checked, he was in critical condition. Needless to say, someone else received the kidney that day, and Nathan's recovery was far from over.

I sat in the waiting room, surrounded by family and pastors. I knew they were disappointed. They wanted this for Nathan, for our family. But I wasn't disappointed. I was angry. After all we have been through as a family, how could this happen? I felt like the psalmist who cries out to God when the wicked seem to prosper while those who follow Him walk through insurmountable troubles. I looked at our precious pastor and said, "We are backed in a corner, and God is going to have to get us out." It was definite that we were in a narrow place and needed breakthrough, but my heart had become hardened during that moment, and I struggled to reconcile our pain.

When Nathan woke up in ICU, I was at one side of the bed and Heather at the other. The doctor and nurse had just removed his breathing tube, and with a smile in his weary eyes. He mustered up the strength to whisper, "Did they do it?"

I choked back tears as I said, "I'm so sorry. Something happened and they weren't able to do the surgery." The overwhelming joy of getting to see him alive after thinking I might have lost my husband overrode my anger. I felt a love for my husband that I had never felt before, love felt in the presence of possible loss. It was deep and emotional, and through my lack of understanding, I had true thankfulness for the Lord that he was alive.

We spent the next week in the hospital. I never left him except for a couple hours one day to shower at a nearby friend's house. He had several more days of intensive care, another surgery to remove blood from around his lungs, and chest tubes in addition to his dialysis. He left the hospital weaker than I had ever seen him. The Lord has always supernaturally sustained him, but this time was hard. His kidneys, that were already barely working on their own, took an even greater hit after the failed surgery. He had multiple battle scars of varying sizes on his chest and abdomen, and he was physically worn down. I realized that as much as I wanted to return to Gabriel and Camila, I would need to stay in the US longer than expected.

Following a long recovery process, I was finally on my way to Honduras. I had a flight to Fort Lauderdale, Florida, and had gotten a shuttle from the airport to a nearby hotel where I would stay until my Honduras flight in the early morning. That was the plan. However, Nathan called and said that he was on his way to the hospital to be treated for peritonitis, an infection in his abdomen. I knew that I had to return to North Carolina and be with him while he fought this serious infection.

Late in the evening, I sent out prayer requests to my closest friends, but I was unprepared for one response I received. It was a critical, deeply crushing response, and the same justice-oriented anger that I had dealt with for the past three months came rushing forth, and a friendship was lost. It felt like in an instant, but then I realized that God had been changing my relationships with people for some time. He was opening some doors and closing others, but I just wanted to hang on. I didn't want any more loss, but the door that I just went through was shut. I mourned and grieved for that relationship for months, and it was the final straw that threw me into almost a year of numbness.

THE BOYLES

There are those with whom you are family, those with whom you become friends, and those whom God puts in your lives for His special purposes. The Boyle family occupies all three of those spaces in our lives. It appears almost every aspect of our relationship was strategic in fulfilling the Lord's purposes. We always enjoyed each other, but I had no idea when we met them in 2014 what we would walk through together, and the decision they made was one that very few are willing to make.

More than a dozen people had selflessly gotten tested to give Nathan a kidney. His transplant coordinator frequently commented on the impressive amount of support. We had several times been close to finding a match, but there would always be a reason why their donation wouldn't be possible. When Todd expressed interest in getting tested himself, I probably shouldn't have been surprised, but after all they had given to our family, I wasn't certain if I wanted him to walk down this road. They had given over and over again to our children, held them when we could not, and now he wanted to give a part of himself to Nathan. He traveled from Honduras to North Carolina to be tested. After several days of testing, he was approved. It was surreal. We finally had a donor for Nathan, and we realized the timing would need to be just as strategic as the moment God brought this family into our lives.

DECISION TIME

Following the three months in the US after Nathan's failed transplant, I pulled up to the gate of my home in Honduras to be greeted by Gabriel and Camila running toward me. I dropped everything I was carrying, and we collided as they knocked me to the ground. They sobbed as Gabriel said repeatedly, "That was too long. That was too long." They held tightly for a while, and I promised them that I would never be gone that long again. My heart was broken, but determination rose above the numbness. I knew that we had to finish this process. We could not stay like this.

I met with my adoption lawyer soon after, and she presented our case to the adoption department of children's services. One of them suggested there were two options to completing these adoptions: we could wait until Nathan received a kidney and then get the referrals, or we could divorce, allowing me to petition as a healthy, single female. As my lawyer told me this, my answer was clear. I immediately said, "No! This is how it is going to work. They are going to give the referrals to us so that Nathan can have a transplant, or they give the referrals to another family, but I will fight for the children." Nathan had been told not to travel for at least a year after transplant because of his immune system, but he would have to travel two times to Honduras to successfully finish the adoptions. We could not wait that long for Nathan's surgery, but those visits were essential. To finish the adoptions now meant that he would have to travel before surgery with his dialysis supplies. It was risky and complicated, but it was decision time. Our lawyer called children's services, and our intentions were made known.

When I went to bed that night, I thought, "What did I just do?" But there was no going back. Gabriel and Camila deserved more. We all did. Breakthrough was needed. After weeks of desperate prayer and waiting, God broke open the way for us. They decided to move our case to committee on the condition that we send in a video of our family along with pictures that showed attachment. We got to work. I was not much of a photographer but compiling a couple dozen photos of our children was easy. Nathan began his homemade video journaling in North Carolina, and it was apparent that there was so much love. I didn't realize at the time how mightily the Lord would use that video to soften hearts.

FINISHING THE RACE

———

TIME OF REFRESHMENT

After returning to Honduras, I realized that our current home would not work for us any longer. After searching a while, we soon found an apartment in the city that would meet our needs and prove to be a refreshing place for our family. It had a pool, playground, and was within walking distance to local restaurants and the grocery store. We were maxing out on credit cards and had drastically cut down our spending as much as we could, but I knew it was a needed change.

Then Todd, while traveling back from NC after getting tested for kidney donation, brought back two amazing gifts: Ethan and Bethany. They were staying for a month, and it became the most refreshing, peaceful time of the entire separation. The summer was full of volleyball, swimming, parks, and zoo visits. I tried to be fully present with them and give them all of me, and I soaked up every moment. We felt the absence of Nathan with us, but supernaturally connected and bonded during that time. Amazingly, it was one of my favorite summers, and I knew God had given me a gift that would break through my numbness and help me to feel again. It was such a tremendous gift that when I returned to Honduras after traveling back to the US for a couple weeks to take Ethan and Bethany back to North Carolina, I was completely heartbroken. I called Nathan while sitting on the tile floor of my apartment bathroom after hours of crying and wanted him to pray for me. I could not stop the tears from flowing, and my heart that was starting to feel again writhed in pain from the separation. We were so close. We were nearing the home stretch, but I felt like I was holding on by my fingernails.

COMMITTEE

The adoption committee of Honduras is made up of physicians, children's advocates, lawyers, social workers, and others who come together regularly to determine adoption outcomes of the children presented to them. They do this outside of their everyday jobs because, as I believe, they have a heart for the most vulnerable. They would need to hear Gabriel and Camila's cases and determine which family or families on the waiting list (both national and international) would be the best match for their specific needs. We never took it for granted that they may not choose us. We prayed and believed they would. We trusted that God, who formed them and knew them more intimately than we did, would do what was best for them.

Eventually, we were visited by two social workers at our Honduran apartment who came to access the physical, social, and mental well-being of the children, our home, and my capacity to care for them. It was a pleasant visit, but afterwards I did not feel confident in the meeting. I felt that there was something working against us, so when they called a couple weeks later to let me know that one of the social workers who had visited us had quit and that they would need to do another visit, I felt somewhat relieved. Our second visit was completely different. I felt immediately that this new worker knew my heart. She could feel my pain, and it became evident that God would use her to help bring this adoption to fruition.

After my adoption lawyer presented the children's cases to the July 18, 2019, committee meeting, she called me. I was driving in downtown Tegucigalpa and quickly pulled over into a Wendy's parking lot. That is when I heard the words, "You got the referrals." I screamed, and anyone who knows me knows that is something I never did. She said that they had watched the video that had been requested and sent in the month beforehand, heard our case and unanimously decided, "How could we ever keep this family apart?" I looked back at my kids in the back seat, with tears streaming down my face I tried to explain to my preschoolers the magnitude of what was unfolding as they intently listened. Hope began to rise again, and I knew that we were going to make it.

SEEING DAD AGAIN

It had been almost two years since Nathan and the kids were separated. The last time Gabriel and Camila had seen Nathan was on the trampoline. We had daily video chats or at least voice messages, but it wasn't the same. He had missed Christmases, birthdays, and their first swims and bike rides, but it was now the time to rebuild what was lost. He would be making his first of two trips to Honduras to finalize the adoptions. It was an overly emotional, exciting time, coupled with the harsh realities of his health. The time required faith, trust, and a strong heart from Nathan and me, and the Lord in His goodness was able to grace us with all.

We had rented a separate hotel room to stay in the two nights Nathan was in Honduras. We were ensured power there for his dialysis machine in case of a city-wide outage, which wasn't uncommon.

They were shy when they saw him again, hiding partially behind me. They did not remember being with him in person, but it didn't take long for them to bond. In the hotel Gabriel, kept hopping up into Nathan's lap, while Camila watched his every move intently. The nights were difficult as Nathan started dialysis in the other bedroom and the children had to stay separate from his sterile equipment. In the mornings, they would meet him with curiosity, questions, and hugs. They were not only experiencing the reality of having a father again, I realized, but they were experiencing their mother loving someone in a new way. They laughed and giggled as Nathan would lean over to give me a kiss and would say, "Do it again." We still wouldn't be reunited completely for a few months, but we all got a glimpse of how wonderful it would be.

CARRYING ME OVER THE FINISH LINE

So many spiritual realities are divinely made known after encountering them firsthand. I now understand that the enemy often attacks you at your place of victory. If he cannot stop the victory itself from occurring, then he will do his best to tarnish it. During the fall of 2019, I slowly allowed the numbness and unresolved pain from the previous spring to alter my judgement, emotions, and the way that I viewed God. I was called to be His daughter, but the trials had only magnified my orphan heart, and I felt alone. I could feel the weight of my flesh and sin closing around me even though we were right at the finish line. I didn't understand why everything felt so heavy and hard when we were now assured the victory, but I needed to finish the race with God, not just for Him.

I called Nathan one evening in November. I was done. I was having a Job moment, and it was real. I cursed the day of my birth. I despised myself. I had no faith left for the little bit that was required, and I was ready to give up. Of course, I knew in reality that I couldn't just stop, but I wanted to. I was in utter despair.

Then, I realized I finally could do no more. He didn't want me to do more. He just wanted my heart. I was humbled, broken, and repentant. In desperate need of a Father, I cried out to Him, and in His faithfulness, He answered. That evening, He began speaking life into me again. I could feel tangible love from Him as He poured out His mercy on me. It was then that He began the process of carrying me over the finish line.

On January 9, 2020, we signed the final adoption decrees. It was a modest hearing with only a few people present at the children's services building. They read eight pages of legal jargon in Spanish while the children squirmed in their seats and occasionally ducked under the table, but it was soon done. Everything seemed rather uneventful considering what we had endured to make it to that moment. I had thought that I would feel something magical in that moment or that something would change within me, but although I fully believe something did change spiritually, I felt the same. I almost felt guilty that I didn't experience the same joy that I experienced at my other children's births or perhaps the joy of other adoptive parents. Then I realized a truth. They were already mine. They were already loved. They were already what the paper outlined from the moment I brought them into my family, but now the world recognized it.

EMBASSY

We were not just eager to be reunited as a family, but we were also racing toward a February 25th deadline to get home before Nathan's transplant. Todd would be flying in a few days prior, and we hoped our entire families would have some much-needed time together to rest before surgery, which would only be possible with a sudden departure date. After the adoption, there remained a list of things that had to be done before we could leave, ranging from obtaining birth certificates to passing medical exams. Lastly, we had to get their visas so they could enter the United States.

February 13th, I had woken up early for our embassy appointment for the necessary visas. I was uneasy because the online portion of the appointment that had to be completed prior to the interviews was not working. The system would not take the children's identification numbers, and unable to rectify the situation, the kids and I went to the embassy despite not having completed all the requirements beforehand. We were able to submit paperwork for the visa petitions but were unable to progress further because of the system glitch. The embassy worked all afternoon remotely to help us fix the problem, and finally, their system took the numbers. I had hoped to get an immediate audience, but they were closing for the day. They told me to come back the next morning, Friday, and gave me an appointment.

The next day, the children and I dressed up once again and went to the embassy with our paperwork in hand. This time, it was approved, and we were called in for our interviews. At the end of the interview, the workers were about to leave when I felt a nudge in my spirit and boldly asked, "I know you all are busy, and I am grateful for all you are doing for our family, but Monday is a holiday, and we are trying to get home before my husband has his kidney transplant on the 25th. What are the chances of getting our passports today?" He smiled kindly at me and asked us to wait while he spoke to someone. He soon came back and said that they would try to get them done that day even though originally they had told us it could take several days.

We left the embassy and drove around, trying not to stray too far. The embassy worker said that they would call when the passports were ready, and we were gone for barely an hour when we got the call to return. We all joyfully marched back into the building as we were handed their visas and asked to look them over. I was mortified to tell the same worker that had been diligently working on our behalf over the past couple days that they had Gabriel's birthday wrong. She was shocked there was an error and commented on how strange it was that there were so many obstacles in getting the children's visas, but they were determined to make it right. We waited in the empty waiting room for about an hour. The kids talked to the guards, we played rock-paper-scissors, and they drew while we waited.

All the sudden we heard cheering break out from behind the closed curtains. *I hope that is for us*, I thought. A few seconds later, grinning from ear to ear, the embassy worker approached and handed us the visas again, and this time they were perfect. It was official. My children and I would be leaving Honduras for the US!

GOING HOME

It was surreal. We had waited over two years for this day, and it was here at last. February 15, 2020, was our homecoming day. It was a day marked with anticipation, joy and even loss as we left the only country Gabriel and Camila had ever known as well as our dear friends and missionary community. We said tearful goodbyes to the

Boyles and our adoption lawyer — all who had fought hard to experience that day with us.

The children were excited but unable to fully grasp what was about to take place. On our first crowded plane ride out of Honduras, I cried the majority of the ride. I still don't even entirely know why I cried, but I think it was mostly due to thankfulness. We had been warring for this day, believing that we would live to see it, yet I was overwhelmed at what the Lord had done.

We flew into Greensboro, NC, and got there around midnight. We were at the top of the escalators coming down to get our baggage when I saw our family waiting on us. At last, we were all together once again. After 2 years, 2 months, and 2 days, our family would be like a family once more. We all knew this was a miracle from God.

TRANSPLANT DAY

Ten days after arriving home, we met Todd's and Nathan's family at the hospital for the transplant. It felt so different coming into this surgery than the last one. There was calmness and peace over everyone, the opposite of what we had experienced almost exactly a year earlier with Nathan's first attempted transplant. I headed back to pre-op with Nathan and Todd as we prayed together and trusted God to sustain their lives. It was a beautiful moment with each other and the Lord, and then Nathan was wheeled back. Heather, after having come for the first surgery, was now with me again as we talked and connected, this time with smiles instead of tears. Most of Nathan's amazing family were there to show love and support, while Todd's parents became like family during our time together. It was such a special time, and I felt this surgery would not end like the last one.

In a few hours, the surgery was done, and I was called up to the receptionist desk to talk to the doctor. "It went great," he said, "They are both doing well." Part of Uncle Todd, as my kids know him, was now inside of my husband, giving him life, and the Giver of Life had orchestrated it all.

RECOVERING ALL

———◆———

THE RESCUE

In my mind, I had envisioned that our recovery would mean getting back all that was lost during the crisis — our families, health, finances. What I didn't realize right away is that the Lord wants to not only bring a recovery of the things that were lost in a particular crisis but also of that the enemy had taken throughout our lives. Even though this was a battle that was won through Christ, He had deeper promises that He wanted to recover with the victory.

> *When David and his men reached Ziklag, they found it destroyed by fire and their wives and sons and daughters taken captive. So David and his men wept aloud until they had no strength left to weep. David's two wives had been captured—Ahinoam of Jezreel and Abigail, the widow of Nabal of Carmel. David was greatly distressed because the men were talking of stoning him; each one was bitter in spirit because of his sons and daughters. But David found strength in the Lord his God. Then David said to*

Abiathar the priest, the son of Ahimelek, "Bring me the ephod." Abiathar brought it to him, and David inquired of the Lord, "Shall I pursue this raiding party? Will I overtake them?" "Pursue them," he answered. "You will certainly overtake them and succeed in the rescue." 1 Samuel 30:3-8 (NIV)

When David and his men returned to camp from the land of the Philistines, they found that their wives and children were taken by the enemy. They were devastated and wept bitterly. They even wanted to stone David and blame him for the enemy's actions. In response, David sought the Lord, and the Lord said, "Pursue them. You will certainly overtake them and succeed in the rescue." David gathered his able-bodied men who were able to fight and pursued the enemy. They fought from dusk until evening the next day, and he recovered ALL that was lost. There was not one thing that had been taken that was missing and he plundered the enemy, saying to the elders of Judah, "Here is a present for you from the plunder of the LORD's enemies" (I Sam. 30:26, NIV).

We are called to have a relationship with God as David did, who was called a man after God's own heart, but we are also called to be warriors. When we finally arrived home as a family, I wanted to rest, and while there was rest for me, it would soon become obvious that the enemy had stolen more than just time, energy, finances. There were deep hurts and fears that had injured me in the fierceness of battle, but the Lord was paving a way for me, just as David, for recovery.

JUST IN TIME

We were already settled in our home in North Carolina as the global pandemic appeared to be gaining strength and making its way into the United States. Within three weeks after Nathan's transplant surgery, the hospital began postponing surgeries. The Honduran government, including its adoption services, closed, and remained closed for over six months. Our life, like many others, came to a screeching halt. I was overwhelmed at the preciseness in which God had orchestrated our adoption, return home, and Nathan's surgery in His perfect timing. He had brought the victory just in time. Three weeks longer and our lives would have been immeasurably harder. The Lord had fought for us, and He won.

We, along with most of the United States, were in lockdown for a season, unable to do life as we were used to doing. Because of Nathan's transplant and weakened immune state, we were isolated further than most, but when it seemed we were losing time, God made it clear to our family that He was restoring lost time. We had been separated for over two years as a family, unable to do so many things together or witness milestones in each other lives, but now we had an opportunity to recover these lost moments. We did not fight our situation. We graciously accepted the fact that our family would be taking a year of furlough after 10 years on the mission field, and we were thankful that other ministry obligations could be done from home. We celebrated an entire year almost solely with each other. We celebrated every birthday together, every holiday together, every up and down. Nathan experienced Gabriel and Camila's first scooter rides, first park experiences, and first lost teeth. There was so much restored in that year, and it took us recognizing God's hand in it to embrace it. It would have been so easy to rush back into "life as normal", but our family was getting something from God that only He, through His unending grace, could give.

TRUST

"We all experience times of testing, which is normal for every human being. But God will be faithful to you. He will screen and filter the severity, nature, and timing of every test or trial you face so that you can bear it. And each test is an opportunity to trust him more, for along with every trial God has provided for you a way of escape that will bring you out of it victoriously." 1 Corinthians 10:13 (TPT)

I knew the feelings that consumed me during the three months following Nathan's unsuccessful surgery would eventually resurface with a vengeance. Everything that I couldn't reconcile about God in that time would have to be dealt with for my heart to recover, and it began to be obvious in my spirit that it came down to trust. Two years of one crisis after another had left me guarding my heart from the only One that I could truly trust with it. Not being able to fully trust the Lord is what had led me to the place of numbness, and I knew that I couldn't stay there.

On April 30, 2020, we, along with most of the world, were still in quarantine. Nathan was gaining strength from his transplant surgery, and the kids were in a wonderful place emotionally despite the circumstances. The kids were upstairs playing while Nathan and I sat on the couch, and I thought about our current reality and our futures. The tears that had been shut up began to flow. I was starting to feel again. I cried with Nathan as I confessed my need for the Lord and professed a need to move into a new season with Him. I needed the Lord to break through my heart of stone and put in me a heart of flesh. It started with me asking Him to forgive me for the anger, bitterness, and expectations I had put on Him, and with it came humility. I felt the love of forgiveness, but I knew that I would be now held to a higher standard to live by, and there would have to be more trust on my part.

Trust is easy when the risks are small. I can easily trust someone to pump my gas or to cut my hair, but the stakes are higher when we are trusting someone with the safety of our life or those we love. That trust should be reserved only for those who are worthy, and God surely is. Unfortunately, I had let Nathan's near-death situation and the stress of the two years diminish my trust in Him. I could still trust Him with some things, but the most important ones were now off limits, such as safety. I lived the past decade of my life taking risks, more than most ever do. We risked our safety, our livelihoods, our friendships, and our financial security. We risked much during our time on the mission field, but it never felt risky. Now, I was back in a "safe" environment in the United States, and suddenly, I was unwilling to take any more risks, but that would change as I began to fully trust Him with my heart again. I felt Him tenderly calling me to become vulnerable to Him and surrender it all.

The Lord's ways are perfect. He has never done anything to break my trust even when I have fallen short and broken His. He is gracious with us and never expects more than we are able to give. I would love to say my trust in Him is complete, but over the past year, He has brought me into new levels of trust I have never even imagined. I can see that although we were not delivered out of every trial, He always made a way of escape and will always be our protector in whom we can trust.

IDENTITY

"For those who are led by the Spirit of God are the children of God. The Spirit you received does not make you slaves, so that you live in fear again; rather, the Spirit you received brought about your adoption to sonship. And by him we cry, "Abba, Father." The Spirit himself testifies with our spirit

that we are God's children. Now if we are children, then we are heirs — heirs of God and co-heirs with Christ, if indeed we share in his sufferings in order that we may also share in his glory." Romans 8:14-17 (NIV)

In the fall of 2020, I was leading an apprenticeship with one of our missionaries in Africa from the US when I was assigned to read a book on spiritual sonship. In 2016, the Lord had started speaking to me about the orphan spirit, a spirit that keeps us in a place of spiritual separation from the Father through perceived rejection. He was wanting me to overcome this spirit in my life completely, but I hadn't fully opened my heart to receiving Him as Father before our tumultuous two years. However, it wasn't long after returning to the US that God made it very clear that He wanted me to recover my full identity as His daughter. Although I had read Romans 8:14 many times before, the Lord was revealing to me more specifically how to apply His Word and allow it to be written upon my heart. I understood that He no longer wanted me to work to save myself because He already had. He wanted to show me His love in new ways, but I had to be willing to receive. I had to be willing to believe in the character of God as a loving Father, gracious, slow to anger, and abounding in mercy. I had to see Him past our human perspective of fathers, which, although sometimes wonderful, can never be an accurate reflection of His love. The day I soaked in this realization, tears ran down my face to the point that my shirt was drenched. I could never move forward in the recovery process as a slave, someone constantly trying to work their way into a place of good standing. I had to rest in knowing that I am His beloved daughter.

I had spent the last two decades of my life wanting to please Him from a place of love, but present within me was also a spirit of self-preservation as I fought to save myself and those I loved. After that day, I started to see the Father differently. Great humility came as I faced the fact that I could not do enough to be His, yet even greater freedom came as the shackles of fear were removed and I no longer endured pressures I once had. The prison wall was broken down by a relentless Father in search of His daughter. Not only did I experience freedom, but the Lord started opening my eyes to my value and who He had called me to be at that time. He has made each of us masterpieces, uniquely made in *His* image, and He is constantly seeing us in our possibilities instead of our failures. This reality brought me to a new place of love, for myself and others, as I embraced the Father's love. I am convinced that this will be a recovery process that will be ongoing and produce more fruit than I can even imagine at this time.

MARRIAGE

This fall (2021) will mark our 20th anniversary. Nathan has been my best friend for a long time. We started dating when I was 16, and I have lived most of my life with him. I don't think I realized how deeply I loved him and how much I relied on him until I lived for most of the two years without him. It was heartbreaking, especially knowing that this was the hardest time of his life too, and his body was failing him.

We were in Petén, a district in Guatemala, for our 10th anniversary. We had just spent the previous year raising funds, selling our possessions, and trading our careers to move to Central America and preach the Gospel. In the middle of doing this, however, we were neglecting each other. During a weekly mentoring session with our directors there, I came in already frustrated. All it took was for them to ask us how everything was going and for my husband to respond with, "Good," for me to muster up a response.

"How can you say we are good? There is nothing good about our situation!" I responded. I had gotten to a dangerous place in our relationship where my spirit wanted reconciliation, but my flesh did not. A year of pouring into everyone else around us and the ministry had drained me dry, but God was gracious to us and planned for our rejuvenation. He sent my Aunt Nancy, who was also our missionary leader, to counsel us, and she led us down the road of forgiveness. It was the support we needed, and that night, Nathan and I confessed our hurts and sins to one another and asked God to help us truly forgive one another. Forgiveness saved our marriage, and since then, we had been growing in our relationship more than ever.

Almost a decade later, we had just made it through another crisis. This time, I didn't hold the same offenses, but the two years of separation had changed me. I had to learn to be both the mother and the father in a foreign land. I had learned to take on all the roles that my husband once occupied. I got the car repaired, I got the home repaired, I got the legal documents, I went to the bank, I did field ministry ... all this I did while caring for my family as before. It was exhausting, and my normally independent nature was pushed to the extreme and it became easy to isolate myself. I realized that although I loved being with Nathan once I returned to the US, when I got upset or angry, my heart turned to the same response: *I don't need you. I can do it myself*. I had learned to do so much by myself, so much I didn't want to do by myself, but I now found difficulty in making myself vulnerable to my husband once again.

The Holy Spirit began to speak to me, and I slowly started to share my heart with him again, praying that he would protect what I was giving him. I had never struggled to give before, but the enemy had taken away a part of my marriage and love for my husband that needed restoration. It started with little things like me allowing him to drive me and the children around. I had to become so vigilant while living under the extreme conditions in Honduras that I no longer felt comfortable with others driving me. I started allowing him to watch the children once he was able. I started letting him back into my heart. It was an intentional decision that did not come easy, but I started seeing the fruits of this choice, and just as ten years before, the Lord began a deep healing. Because of Him, our marriage prospered more than ever before. We came out of that season appreciating the deep love that's formed through the hard places in life. We were wounded, but not defeated. There are many treasures that are created on the battlefield, but it takes healing to discover what you've gained after the smoke has cleared. I look forward to more recovery in this area as the Lord continues to move us both deeper in our relationship with Him.

INHERITANCE

"Through our union with Christ we too have been claimed by God as his own inheritance. Before we were even born, he gave us our destiny; that we would fulfill the plan of God who always accomplishes every purpose and plan in his heart." Ephesians 1:11 (TPT)

God is a God of family. He is a fierce protector of family, as each of us were destined from the beginning to be His family and inheritance, so that might fulfill every plan for His wonderful purpose. When Gabriel and Camila were infants, we frequently prayed scripture and declared their destinies over them. I really didn't know their backgrounds entirely, but I knew that there was an enemy who wanted to stop generational change. That is why the adoptions were met with such resistance. The adoptions didn't just change Gabriel and Camila's futures. It changed their succeeding generations. In the same way, I knew that our family's decision to take the harder road would change not only our futures but those of our generations.

I had often believed that Gabriel and Camila would respond differently to life once they were in a place of permanency. I wasn't sure what that would look like, but

I felt that once they were no longer in limbo, some of the struggles that looked fierce at the time would not be so hard once we were reunited. That was truly an understatement. Within a month of being home, Gabriel and Camila were changing drastically. Gabriel, who had made tremendous progress with anger the year before coming home, was now going days, weeks, without angry outbursts. His impulsivity lessened, his self-control increased, and he was at peace. Camila, who often hid her face in moments of confrontation or lashed out in passive-aggressive behaviors, was now confident, secure, laughing, and quick to listen. The Lord had helped me learn how to parent them in a way that honored them, me, and Him, and it was all a part of His continuous recovery.

On October 7, 2020, I was outside in the back yard with Gabriel and Camila as they played. They were running around when Gabe stopped in his tracks and walked up to me. He said, "Mom, would you pray with me to ask Jesus into my heart?" It came out of nowhere. We often talked about Jesus, but I had never asked him to receive salvation. But he was ready. Then Camila walked up and said the same thing, so in the back yard I prayed with them as their lives were changed forever. The next week, Nathan baptized both of them in the bathtub.

Ethan, my firstborn who was about to graduate from high school, has always been a delight. He is gentle, wise, and righteous, an old soul. I have learned so much through watching him. I started rekindling my relationship with him and enjoying the time that I now had to invest into him. We talked for hours at any opportunity we could get. We talked while making supper, while outside, while watching the kids play. It was amazing, and it was almost entirely centered around the Lord. He wanted to know more about Him; he craved knowledge, understanding, and an experience with Him. My son, who had accepted Jesus as his Savior at 8 years old, had now found his first love. Bethany started changing, too. Worldly things didn't capture her attention anymore. She became lighter and freer, and I knew God was working in her.

Then we decided to have worship nights for the Lord. We didn't want to make it something to just check off the box. Our family was ready and hungry for God. The first couple of days started out hard with the young kids not wanting to participate or falling asleep during the worship, but then something shifted. The Spirit of God stirred our hearts, and we were all in. Over the next several months, our children were filled with the Holy Spirit, made holy declarations, and prayed fervently during worship. They looked forward to what God was doing, and I saw that God Himself was placing his truths inside of them. He is recovering my children, each one of them, to Himself. I have confidence that this will only be the beginning of seeing destinies fulfilled in my children's lives as they live for Him and make Him their portion.

Atwood Family Declaration

In the name of Jesus, I declare that our family will live as a testimony of the Lord's goodness. He will speak His words through the actions of our family. There is a grace and covering over our family that will be told through the generations. The Lord will go before us as a mighty wind, forcibly removing all snares in our path. Our mouths will minister to the peoples of all nations. We will move with the Spirit of God where He sends us. We will be ready in season and out of season to share the wonderful works and glorious nature of our Father in Heaven. We will be as the mighty oak trees, rooted and grounded in the Word, steadfast and immoveable, unscathed when storms come and yet our leaves gently moving to the breeze of the Holy Spirit. Our refreshing will come from the River of Life, in whom we will never thirst. The righteousness of the Lord will go before us with His glory our rearguard. We are protected and secure from the harm of the enemy, and where our feet tread, there will be great favor among the people and the nations. The love of God will be our strength, and out of that will flow miracles and wonders that bring glory to our Father in Heaven. We will be as generations of Levitical priests, called apart for God's holy purposes, His divine pleasure, to minister to Him, and then to the people of the nations. We have been called to set the captive free and bring liberty to the lands that have been enslaved. We will break the chains that are ensnaring God's people in Jesus' name, and they will be released to their true destinies in Christ. We will be the head and not the tail. We will prosper and be in health, even as our souls prosper. We will hide in the shadow of His wing and yet soar as eagles. We are called to a holy place, to dwell in His presence, and to draw others into that same place. We will minister throughout the generations in the perfect will of our Father, giving glory and honor to Him always. We are His and He is ours.

PEACE

After being home for seven months, I hit a wall. Nathan and I had just come out of a time of repentance, prayer, and fasting when one more morning I woke up with extreme anxiety. Thoughts flooded my mind of every possibly horrible situation that could happen in my life. I had dealt with anxiety and depression in the past, but nothing like this. I thought at the time that it was the enemy tormenting me, and perhaps it partly was. However, I now know that it was God allowing what had been hidden to come to the surface so that I would find healing and peace in Him.

The anxiety was so debilitating that I stayed in my bed for a week, unable to function. I could hardly eat. I was nauseous, my blood pressure was elevated, my heart was beating out of my chest constantly, and I felt like I was going to die. I couldn't even message my family or friends to pray for me, it was too much. Finally, after a week of suffering, I kissed Nathan and the children, got my keys, insurance card, debit card, and Bible, and told my husband I would be back later. The truth was, I didn't know if I was coming back. I had told the Lord that I couldn't take any more and that either He would have to heal me, or I was going to check myself in for psychiatric care.

I started driving, just driving. About ten minutes into the car ride, I started wailing and groaning as the Holy Spirit was doing a deep work. I soon pulled over into a church parking lot, seated on the outskirts of town, and began praying. The Lord started revealing to me areas that had been wounded during the battle and never properly healed. I received healing and truth as I repented for believing the enemy's lies and for allowing them to continue hurting me. I wrote down His words on a piece of paper, knowing that the real work would begin as I allowed Him to renew my mind with His truths. After a couple hours I felt a release to go home. The next day, I woke up anxious again, so I got up and did that whole routine all over. The following day, it happened again. My husband, who had been fasting and praying for me, anointed me with oil, and the anxiety lessened enough for me to sleep. The next day, I went to meet with Dr. Kathy.

Dr. Kathy, Christian counselor and friend, met with me, and together, we began to achieve breakthrough. I thought my anxiety was from the two years of crisis catching up to me, but that was only part of it. God was wanting me to recover more than what was lost during that time. He wanted me to recover ALL that had been lost. The conversation took a turn to my younger self, twelve-year-old Alison. This Alison experienced a year that changed her. Her parents separated, and her father moved away. Her grandmother died. She changed schools three times. She was harassed, bullied, and beaten up, and she had a knife pulled on her. She was molested. She had her house robbed while she slept upstairs. Her uncle committed murder, and she helped clean up the bloodstained house. It left her scarred and vulnerable. She was terrified of making a mistake. She felt unprotected and that everything was out of her control. She felt unable to protect those around her. She felt like she would never be ready or qualified to handle a crisis but always expecting the next one. And none of that came to the surface until a crisis of equal magnitude arose.

Then began the recovery process that brought back plunder from the enemy that had long been captured. It started with a simple question from Dr. Kathy. We were talking about my thoughts and taking them captive, not allowing myself to relive situations continually in my mind, not allowing condemnation to take hold, and not obsessing over mistakes or potential crisis situations. I said I didn't want to continue these things, to which she replied, "Then why are you allowing it?" She was right. I had allowed these thoughts to unknowingly possess my mind for over twenty years and felt like a victim of my circumstances, unable to change the outcome. But in that moment, I understood and had a clear revelation of the healing that God wanted for me, and it was time.

We all want things to be easy. We want to be able to pray once or even a few times and expect the enemy to give up without a fight. Sometimes God does do a miraculous work instantly, but I have found it usually doesn't work that way, especially with matters regarding the soul. It takes time. It takes determination. It takes dying to the flesh, but most of all, it takes us letting God be Lord over our lives and let Him do the work that only He can do. Over the next six months, His truths that were once hard to entertain were becoming a part of me. The thoughts that I once had to take captive every fifteen minutes or so became less frequent and eventually faded. The scriptures that I had hung on my wall to read aloud every time the enemy came became written on my heart. He was taking me from glory to glory and re-establishing peace in my heart, peace I hadn't held in a long time.

FREEDOM

"You've gone into my future to prepare the way, and in kindness you follow behind me to spare me from the harm of my past. You have laid your hand on me!" Psalm 139:5 (TPT)

I often felt guilt for not feeling victorious after the Lord had overcome such obstacles in our lives. I knew we had gotten over the finish line, but I didn't feel like a winner.

I felt damaged. A picture of myself in armor would frequent my mind. I had just finished the battle and pushed the enemy army back, but there were gashes all over my body where the enemy had pierced the armor. I was crawling when I felt like I should be gallantly striding.

In the months following being reunited and Nathan's transplant, I began noticing that I was unable to get out of the past. Things I hadn't thought about or processed in the middle of the battle were then consuming my thoughts. I felt such regret. *I should have done it better. I should have been aware of the enemy's schemes. I should have been more like Christ in that moment.* There were a million should-haves. I didn't want to talk about the two years. I didn't want to look at pictures. All I saw was a past that defined me, and the enemy had convinced me that it was all bad. That was a lie. The reality is it is very easy to know what we should have done after the fact, and when we do all the should-haves, we are holding ourselves up to unrealistic expectations that God doesn't expects us to follow. Those are the moments when we must choose forgiveness and hold tight to His promises, as tight as we do for our next breathe.

"Whenever our hearts make us feel guilty and remind us of our failures, we know that God is much greater and more merciful than our conscience, and he knows everything there is to know about us. My delightfully loved friends, when our hearts don't condemn us, we have a bold freedom to speak face-to-face with God. And whatever we ask of him we receive, because we keep his commands. And by our beautiful intentions we continue to do what brings pleasure to him." 1 John 3:20-22 (TPT)

I decided to visit a lake. My dad and I had loved to visit a particular part of this lake near our home. I grew up on a creek, so I remember having a fishing rod from about the time I could walk. As a matter of fact, the earliest picture I have with my dad is from a day when we went fishing. So, I thought it was appropriate that I would visit one of our old spots for healing. I had made up my mind that I wasn't going to keep letting the past define me — failures, regrets, hurts. I was tired of living in the past, and I was ready to let go. When I got to the lake, I found several smooth stones and rocks and sat down at a picnic table with my marker and my Bible. I started writing people's names on the rocks, forgiving those who had hurt me during those two years. Most I had already forgiven, but this time I was throwing my offenses into the lake where it would sink to the bottom, never to be retrieved again. I prayed, forgave, and threw the rocks one by one until I got to the last and biggest one. Actually, it was part of a brick. It was heavy, and my name was written upon it. I was choosing to forgive myself, and I knew I had made a declaration before God that I would not try to fish it out. I dropped it in, and I breathed deeply as the water from the splash dewed my face. It was healing, and it was freedom that the Lord helped me to recover.

GOING BACK THE WAY I CAME

"The Lord said to him, "Go back the way you came, and go to the Desert of Damascus. When you get there, anoint Hazael king over Aram. Also, anoint Jehu son of Nimshi king over Israel, and anoint Elisha son of Shaphat from Abel Meholah to succeed you as prophet. Jehu will put to death any who escape the sword of Hazael, and Elisha will put to death any who escape the sword of Jehu. Yet I reserve seven thousand in Israel—all whose knees have not bowed down to Baal and whose mouths have not kissed him." 1 Kings 19:15-18 (NIV)

Six months after hitting the wall that led me into transformation, I got stuck again. I could feel the anxiety rising within me, and I started feeling like I needed to walk. So, I began walking a lot. I got out into the fresh air, prayed, and hit breakthrough every day. It seemed like the healing process was accelerated, and for every thought and lie that the enemy threw at me, the Lord gave me a truth. It was exhausting, but it began to expose the enemy's condemnation, which masqueraded as conviction from God. I spent the next several days refusing to entertain the ungodly thoughts that came and rebuking them, but it was still a fight, and I felt like spinning wheels. I took several days for myself to hear from the Lord, and He spoke to me about Elijah. In 2017, He had told me to rest and eat because the journey would be too much for me. This time, I heard him say, "Why are you here?"

I read through 1 Kings again, and Elijah's story gripped me deeply. He had just won a tremendous victory for the Lord. He had honored and glorified the Lord in the company of Baal's prophets and was supernaturally filled with the Spirit of God to even run ahead of the king after the showdown on their return to Jezreel. So why was he overcome with fear after Jezebel threatened to kill him? After all, he had just seen the miraculous power of the Lord with his very eyes. He was so afraid that he ran to the next town and then a day's journey into the desert before he collapsed. It was then that God sent an angel to feed him and give him water while he rested.

After this encounter, Elijah traveled forty days to Mount Horeb for God to ask, "Why are you here?"

I knew when God asked me the same question, he was asking why I was hiding in fear. My heart will ever be filled with compassion for what Elijah went through because I understand. When you take a great stand for the Lord, even in your victory, the enemy will attempt to devour all that he can, even if it isn't the victory itself. He will use fear to do it. Elijah was experiencing real warfare, and so do all who choose to answer God's calling on their lives. However, God has the solution. He is the solution, but He cannot share thrones with anyone else in our lives for us to gain the full victory in this area. I realized I had to throw down two other thrones in my life down that were equal to God's, and these were set up for fear and myself. It was time to dethrone them both so that God alone would be enthroned in my life.

As my simple prayers of declaration rang out, His power and life filled me. I buried my face in the carpeted rug of my bedroom floor and waited for His whisper. I waited for His instructions. Then the Lord gave me a vision. It was my open, broad place from Psalm 18, the place where there is safety, security, and blessing, and around me was a wall. It was a fortified wall. It was God's hedge of protection, sealed by the blood of Christ. I knew that everything within me that had set itself up against Him was thrown over the wall. I threw it over when I prayed. He also spoke to me to keep the enemy out and to not let him return. When we choose to partner with the enemy and believe his lies, we create holes in our walls in which the enemy can come in and steal God's blessings. I received an intense desire to keep the enemy out and for my wall to be secure and believed God would give me grace to accomplish this. Almost immediately, I started to feel joy return to my life. Dread turned to excitement, anxiety turned to peace, and I knew this was big. He wasn't just recovering treasures. He was recovering thrones.

Over the next two days, I heard loudly in my spirit, "Go back the way you came." I didn't know what exactly that meant, so I prayed, and the Lord reminded me of my next assignment: to write. In going back through the time of life that was the most painful for me, choosing to relive and retell a story that is not just mine but His was healing. Writing this book was healing. It allowed me to go back the way I came. Elijah dethroned fear when he acknowledged God's glory and majesty, covered his face, and came into His presence. Because I did the same, my walk back through the desert was much different this time, one filled with grace, peace, an assignment, and a promise of inheritance and recovery.

MORE TO COME

"And without faith living within us it would be impossible to please God. For we come to God in faith knowing that he is real and that he rewards the faith of those who passionately seek him." Hebrews 11:6 (TPT)

Although many people would look at our lives and think that we have an abundance of faith, the reality is most people have faith that is stronger in some areas than others, and it grows in our walk with the Lord. When we first became Christians, we were young and barely making it financially. Once we realized that tithing was required for obedience, it took a new level of faith. We realized that God is and will always be faithful to His word, and we started developing faith for greater things. Believing that God would do what He said He would do kept me going for two years of brutal living conditions. In the recovery process, I realized my faith would have to rise once again to believe that He is a rewarder of those who seek Him. I had to believe that He wants me to receive as much as He wants me to give, and He wants to reward me more than He wants to correct me. I had to have faith to believe in His true character despite what circumstances, emotions, and other people said about Him. There will continue to be more situations in our lives that will require greater levels of faith than I currently have; however, even our faith is a grace gift from Him. As I remember His truths and surrender myself fully to Him, recovery will continue, and there will be more to come.

BUILDING RESILIENCE

I am sure I am like many others by believing it is easy to concentrate on the positives in order to ignore the negatives. I originally did not want to add this last section. In fact, it took me a whole new journey with the Lord and revelation to realize that it needed to be added. As we allow the Lord to build resilience in our lives, letting Him take us from glory to glory and mold us in His image, we must realize that suffering is inevitable.

I was sitting outside my mother-in-law's house as she graciously offered to care for my children while my husband underwent needed hip replacement surgeries. We hadn't decided that we would opt for more surgeries at that time, and I wasn't sure that I could emotionally handle the idea of more surgeries so soon. But I felt the Lord stirring my spirit, and as I watched my forty-three-year-old husband walk around the house with a cane, which he had been doing for the past several months, a picture flooded my mind. It was a picture of a mighty oak tree with deep roots being blown around fiercely in the middle of a storm with raging winds and rain. The oak was bending, but it wasn't breaking. It was resilient. And then something that I knew all along settled into my spirit. ***You cannot be resilient without having overcome significant trials and crises in your life.***

This realization lead us to go through a successful right hip replacement with a left one in the works. Of course, we would have liked the Lord to have miraculously given him new hips, and we believed for it, just like we believed for a new kidney. In all these times, God did provide for us what we needed, just not in the easy way or the way we thought he would work. Nonetheless, He was and will always be a good and faithful Father. That truth is based on His nature, not on our circumstances. If most of us had it our way, we would never go through hard times. We would never need to war for anything. We would never have disease, sickness, or death. We would immediately be delivered out of every hard situation. The reality is that is what God wanted for us too. That is His heart for us, but as followers of Christ we live in a world that is constantly at odds with the Holy Spirit that lives within us, and we have to be a resilient people with deep roots. We are called to live like Jesus.

Although we must have faith to please God, we can often let "faith" keep us from seeing the bigger picture of what God is doing in our lives. This is what happened to Peter. When Jesus began to unveil the Father's plan of His death, Peter could not see the bigger picture. He did not realize that the suffering and sacrifice would make a way for redemption of all humanity. All he saw was the way he believed things should be, and after trying to "correct" his master, Jesus rebuked him. Often, we can try to avoid trials or crises, pretending they don't exist or failing to acknowledge them, yet we are guaranteed suffering in this life. We will all have times in our lives when we feel grief, sadness, and loss, but it will not always be for lack of faith. Many times, it will be the opposite. It will be because we are called to a life like Jesus. However, we are reminded of his truth in Romans 8:17 (NIV):

"Now if we are children, then we are heirs, heirs with Christ, if indeed we share in his sufferings in order that we may also share in his glory."

The good news is we have the Advocate, the Healer, the Restorer who is constantly working on our behalf to see to it that we succeed. He believes in us much more than we do ourselves, and there is nothing that is given up for Him that is not given back unto us. There will be things that will never be fully recovered in this life because of the world that we live in, but we can be thankful that those who finish their lives with Christ Jesus will obtain the fullness of their salvation, and in doing so, they will recover ALL.

Made in the USA
Columbia, SC
24 October 2021